DATE DUE

DE _ 7 00			

DEMCO 38-296

Roland Barthes on Photography

Roland Barthes

Crosscurrents
Comparative Studies in
European Literature and Philosophy

University Press of Florida
Gainesville • Tallahassee • Tampa • Baca Raton
Pensacola • Orlando • Miami • Jacksonville

on Photography

The Critical Tradition in Perspective

Nancy M. Shawcross

Crosscurrents

Comparative Studies in European Literature and Philosophy

Edited by S. E. Gontarski

Improvisations on Michel Butor: Transformation of Writing, by Michel Butor; edited, annotated, and
    with an introduction by Lois Oppenheim; translated by Elinor S. Miller (1996).
The French New Autobiographies: Sarraute, Duras, and Robbe-Grillet, by Jean-Michel Rabaté (1996).
Carlo Emilio Gadda and the Modern Macaronic, by Albert Sbragia (1996).
Roland Barthes on Photography: The Critical Tradition in Perspective, by Nancy M. Shawcross (1997).

———————————

02 01 00 99 98 97 6 5 4 3 2 1

Epigraph: Cariature by Honoré Daumier of a man in a headrest for a pose, no date. Nadar Album,
Special Collections, Van Pelt Library, University of Pennsylvania.

Library of Congress Cataloging-in-Publication Data

Shawcross, Nancy M.
    Roland Barthes on photography: the critical tradition in perspective / Nancy M. Shawcross.
    p. cm. — (Crosscurrents)
    Includes bibliographical references and index.
    ISBN 0-8130-1469-7
    1. Photography—Philosophy. 2. Photographic criticism. 3. Barthes, Roland. I. Title.
II. Series: Crosscurrents (Gainesville, Fla.)
TR183.S43   1997   96-26838
770'.1—dc20

The University Press of Florida is the scholarly publishing agency for the State University System
of Florida, comprised of Florida A & M University, Florida Atlantic University, Florida International University, Florida State University, University of Central Florida, University of Florida,
University of North Florida, University of South Florida, and University of West Florida.

University Press of Florida
15 Northwest 15th Street
Gainesville, FL 32611

for Spencer *always*

Contents

Preface

The age of mechanical reproduction begins with photography. Its discovery not only stands as one of the most important and signature events of the Industrial Revolution, it represents the first *analog* medium, predating recorded sound by nearly forty years and the motion picture by over half a century. Unlike a metaphor that seeks its connection with a subject in terms of an imaginary resemblance, the photograph functions like a metonym, which draws its figurative expression directly from the object, usually from some part of its physical characteristics. The process, therefore, of transformation is an inherently limited one in photography; some physical phenomenon will have always *preceded* the photographic image. Whatever "art" may be rhetorically grafted onto a photographic print by photographer or critic, it can never completely eliminate the photograph's literal connection with reality. André Bazin made a similar observation concerning the motion picture in 1956: "Cinema attains its fullness in being the art of the real" (quoted in Andrew 1976, 137). In *What Is Cinema?* he iterates his position that cinema's realism is "not certainly the realism of subject matter or realism of expression, but that realism of space without which moving pictures do not constitute cinema" (Bazin 1967, 1:112).

In the musings and critical writings on photography in the past 155 years, a dichotomy of terms has emerged. In the following list the photograph— for better or worse, depending on the critic—has been associated with nomenclature contextualized, more often than not, in a binary opposition to art and the imagination.

The Photograph	*Its Counterpoint*
metonym	metaphor
reality	art

authoritative	transcendent
transliteration	transformation
denotation	connotation
witness (a report)	seer (representing expressive genius or having spiritual significance)
concrete	abstract
informational	contemplative/representational

As Jacques Derrida has argued in his analysis of Western metaphysics, such binary oppositions privilege one value over the other. A hierarchy between terms is implicit and gives priority to one at the expense of the other. Western theories of art—particularly those developed throughout the nineteenth century and whose shorthand label reads "art for art's sake"—emphasize the importance of imagination and the insight or genius of the artist. So dominant has this philosophy of art been that literary criticism in academe throughout the better part of the twentieth century has tended to privilege literature of complexity and imagination over realism.

Modern critical theory—such as the work of F. R. Leavis and the Cambridge School or its American counterpart known as New Criticism—valued and therefore promoted the study of the aesthetic qualities of a work—its verbal complexities and subtleties in and of themselves. In contradistinction to this critical trend was the appropriation in the 1950s of semiotics/semiology from the field of linguistics and structuralism from that of anthropology as critical methodologies for literature. Among the results of the adoption or consideration of these critical approaches was a deemphasis on the *aesthetic quality or value* of the work in an interest to analyze and understand how communication is structured and what message is being conveyed. Roland Barthes represents one of the key popularizers of semiology as a methodological approach for literary studies, beginning with his essay "Myth Today" in the 1957 publication of *Mythologies* and continuing throughout the 1960s in dozens of publications and presentations. Barthes originally developed his ideas on semiology and structuralism principally from the work of Swiss linguist Ferdinand de Saussure and French anthropologist Claude Lévi-Strauss. After the objectivity of these theories was challenged by Derrida (beginning with his 1966 conference paper, "Structure, Sign, and Play in the Discourse of the Human Sciences"), Barthes drifted away from a strictly formal application of structuralist techniques for both literary and cultural analyses. In the midst of these developments and alterations in critical methodology, the photograph remained as a vexing entity that both intrigued and at times irritated Barthes.

Roland Barthes's only book-length monograph on photography—*La chambre claire: Note sur la photographie* [Camera lucida: reflections on photography]—happens also to be the author's last publication in his lifetime. It represents a culminating statement by Barthes on the subject of photography—culminating both in concept and tone. Yet the text remains perplexing both in and of itself and in relation to nearly thirty years of Barthes's intermittent writing on the image and on the photograph in particular. According to Gabriel Bauret in an essay that appeared in *Roland Barthes et la photo: Le pire des signes* (1990), "this book is the most paradoxical that has ever been written on photography" (13) (author's translation).

The study of the history, criticism, and theory of photography is a relatively new and eccentric discipline. Many commentators of the past two decades have lamented this fact and have looked to Barthes either to defend or define their positions in an inchoate field. Allan Sekula and Estelle Jussim, for example, refer to Barthes's early writings on photography to introduce or elaborate upon the political implications and uses of photography. The appearance of *La chambre claire* in 1980 and its English translation, *Camera Lucida,* in 1981 generated great excitement and anticipation in the photographic community. Yet frequent in the reviews and in subsequent citations of the work is a sense of disappointment that Barthes's essay does not address the writer's particular philosophic or aesthetic concern regarding the medium of photography. Andy Grundberg, for example, who was the reviewer of *Camera Lucida* for *The New York Times Book Review,* stated:

> The posthumous publication of Roland Barthes's thoughts on the medium [of photography] raises unusually high expectations. . . . "Camera Lucida" is not, however, the definitive reappraisal of photography that was anticipated. It does not reveal the long-sought "grammar" of photographs. (23 August 1981, page 11)

In a 1981 article for the *Village Voice,* which was reprinted in *The Privileged Eye: Essays on Photography* (1987), Max Kozloff states that he respects Barthes's "amused consciousness" and is even moved by it, but the text leaves him wanting more. He contends that the work contains no "reasoning about the social and historical placement of its objects. So there is a failure of empathy at the core of a book that stresses empathic perception, and with that, a failure of aesthetic response as well" (248). As early as 1982 some found it time to offer a "re-reading" of *Camera Lucida*. Victor Burgin, for example, sets his task:

> to provide a (re-)reading of Barthes's work on photography which pays attention both to the "fraying" of his text (where "his" meanings "edge out"' into the sea of intertextuality), and to their structure (consistency of analytic "motifs," and their patterning, repetitions, transformations, across the totality of his work). (Burgin 1986, 75)

Yet as multifarious and informed as Burgin's rereading appears, it seeks its paths of inquiry more in the literal or denotative explication of Barthes's dedication and marginal references and less in the more ambiguous system of intertextuality that may, in fact, represent Barthes's true sense of "quotation" within his texts.

In general, there has been some difficulty meshing Barthes's analysis of photography prior to *Camera Lucida* with the expression contained in *Camera Lucida*. Focusing first on this last text and then looking backward to its sources, the complexity and integrity of Barthes's ideas on photography. Although *Camera Lucida* remains an essay on photography, it is informed by philosophical and cultural perspectives that invite a more complicated reading than is often the case. Barthes approaches his assignment—his investigation of photography—from a blend of interests and with a methodology uniquely his: he partakes of many image-repertoires. What he most fears is that the Image (that is, a *single* image) will dominate and oppress, so he suggests that one way, perhaps, to thwart the Image is to corrupt languages, vocabularies. "The proof that one has succeeded is the indignation, the reprobation of purists, of specialists. I cite the Others, even as I distort them; I shift the meaning of words" (RL 357). He advocates "suspension of Images" while maintaining that "suspension is not negation" (RL 356).

Roland Barthes on Photography: The Critical Tradition in Perspective approaches the explication of Barthes's ideas on photography through the explication of his last essay on the subject, *Camera Lucida*. *Camera Lucida* remains a complex, paradoxical, and elusive text for those seeking a reading on the medium of photography. Barthes's earlier remarks on photography, however, have been extensively evaluated and incorporated into the critical discourse of the medium. The pervasive citation of *Mythologies*, "The Photographic Message," and "Rhetoric of the Image" for the past twenty years in writings on photography may have impeded the photographic community's immediate embrace of and coming to terms with *Camera Lucida*. The concept of intertextuality underlies Barthes's methodological approach to writing about photography in *Camera Lucida*. Figuratively speaking, *Camera Lucida* is a palimpsest in which various intertexts reside. Interaction between these texts moves in several directions, not simply the direction of past onto present. The elucidation of this text reanimates the earlier writing in a way that a strictly chronological discussion of Barthes's writings would inhibit. Of equal importance is the reevaluation of several classic texts on photography that inform the Western world's ideas on the medium. They include, in particular, Charles Baudelaire's "Salon de 1859" review and several of Walter Benjamin's essays, including "A Short History of Photography" and "The Work of Art in the Age of Mechanical Reproduction."

Among the intertexts or image-repertoires at play in *Camera Lucida* are (1) the legacy found within Barthes's own texts, some of which pertain to the medium of photography explicitly and some of which regard the photograph obliquely; (2) the novelty of the photograph in the first two decades of its public existence and how it informs the mythologies by which Barthes begins his "ontological" search to learn what photography is "in itself"; (3) the writings of Charles Baudelaire and the complexity of his views on photography; (4) the contextualization of Barthes's ideas through the "third form," a genre that partakes of both the essay and the novel; and (5) time as photography's *punctum* as understood through discussions of time and light in modern physics. Through the window of *Camera Lucida* Barthes's unique vision of the medium of photography is fully framed. In addition, through the perspective of Barthes's views on photography the historical debate on the medium is refocused.

There were many encouraging and helpful individuals who made possible this publication. Initially, I would like to thank Walda Metcalf, Editor-in-Chief of the University Press of Florida, who remained committed to this project from beginning to end. My respect and appreciation extend particularly to Jean-Michel Rabaté, Gerald Prince, Dorothy Noyes, and Craig Saper, all of the University of Pennsylvania, for their unflagging support and expert counsel. The loyalty, encouragement, and patience of Faye McMahon and Bettsy Mosimann contributed immeasurably to my work. Rebecca Smith provided remarkable care and attention to proofreading the text. Additionally, I wish to acknowledge the professionalism and considerate assistance of the members of the Interlibrary Loan Department in Van Pelt Library and of the Fisher Fine Arts Library, University of Pennsylvania, in particular Lee Pugh, Tom Schnepp, Joe McCloskey, and Alan Morrison.

Abbreviations

CL   *Camera Lucida: Reflections on Photography.* Translated by Richard Howard. New York: Hill and Wang, 1981.

ES   *Empire of Signs.* Translated by Richard Howard. New York: Hill and Wang, 1983.

GV   *The Grain of the Voice: Interviews 1962–1980.* Translated by Linda Coverdale. New York: Hill and Wang, 1985.

MI   *Michelet.* Translated by Richard Howard. New York: Hill and Wang, 1987.

MY   *Mythologies.* Selected and translated by Annette Lavers. New York: Hill and Wang, 1972.

RB   *Roland Barthes by Roland Barthes.* Translated by Richard Howard. New York: Hill and Wang, 1977.

RF   *The Responsibility of Forms.* Translated by Richard Howard. New York: Hill and Wang, 1985.

RL   *The Rustle of Language.* Translated by Richard Howard. New York: Hill and Wang, 1986.

S/Z   *S/Z.* Translated by Richard Miller. New York: Hill and Wang, 1974.

WDZ   *Writing Degree Zero.* Translated by Annette Lavers and Colin Smith. New York: Hill and Wang, 1977.

then a device was invented, a kind of prosthesis
invisible to the lens, which supported and main-
tained the body in its passage to immobility:
this headrest was the pedestal of the statue
I would become, the corset of my imaginary essence.—Roland Barthes,
Camera Lucida

1. Beyond the Photograph as Sign

> If we were to choose a photographer to have been at Golgotha, or walking the streets of Rome during the sacking, who would it be? Numerous photographers have been trained to get the picture, and many leave their mark on the picture they get. For that moment of history, or any other, I would personally prefer that the photograph was stamped *Photographer Unknown*. This would assure me, rightly or wrongly, that I was seeing a fragment of life, a moment of time, as it was. The photographer who has no hand to hide will conceal it with the least difficulty. Rather than admiration for work well done, I will feel the awe of revelation. The lost found, the irretrievable retrieved.
>
> Wright Morris, "In Our Image"

Until his untimely death in 1980, Roland Barthes's professional writing career spanned more than three decades. Throughout this time Barthes sporadically offered commentary about the medium of photography. In the 1950s he produced several pieces regarding photography that were later collected in *Mythologies,* for example, "Photos-Chocs," "Photography and Electoral Appeal," and "The Great Family of Man." In 1961, nineteen years prior to the publication of *La chambre claire* (*Camera Lucida* in its English-language translation of 1981), Barthes wrote an essay on photography entitled "The Photographic Message." Additional interviews and references in other published works attest to a persistent interest in the photograph. They reveal a development of thought or perspective on the photograph that culminates at first in the attempt to decipher photographic images as signs but which ultimately moves away from such concerns and follows a provocative, albeit highly individualistic, path.

What are Barthes's concerns with regard to the medium of photography? The text of *Camera Lucida* begins with the appearance that Barthes is unresolved as to whether photography *exists* and is struggling to understand and systematize its quiddity. In comparison, an essay such as "The Photographic Message" appears relatively straightforward in its explication of the medium and its import, because it concerns itself, for the most part, with a specific type of photograph: the press photograph. Examined over a thirty-year period, however, Barthes's writing and analyses do not remain the same: they branch and evolve. His quest in the 1950s to develop and promote a method of cultural study called semiology differs somewhat from the 1960s, and by the 1970s Barthes's intellectual preoccupations have distinctly changed in terms of his methodology. Prior to *Camera Lucida* Barthes's approaches to photography can be characterized as being "first ideological (*Mythologies*), then semiological (the study of the various photographic messages)" (Gilles Mora in *Roland Barthes et la photo,* 1990; author's translation).

The 1957 afterword of *Mythologies* lays out a methodology for understanding myth that informs both Barthes's ideological and semiological treatises on photography. Its heart is the recognition that structurally a myth (which is a system of communication, according to Barthes) comprises interdependent layers of signs and meanings: the relation between signifier and signified creates an entity that he calls sign, which then becomes signifier in the next link of the structural chain relating to myth. Myth, therefore, eliminates or supersedes variety among the media that initiate its structural chain and transforms the physical differences inherent in the raw materials into the same functional essence as sign or meaning in the next link.

> We must here recall that the materials of mythical speech (the language itself, photography, painting, posters, rituals, objects, etc.), however different at the start, are reduced to a pure signifying function as soon as they are caught by myth. Myth sees in them only the same raw material; their unity is that they all come down to the status of a mere language. Whether it deals with alphabetical or pictorial writing, myth wants to see in them only a sum of signs, a global sign, the final term of a first semiological chain. (MY 114)

Thus Barthes's initial view of photography carries no depth—no sense of the inherent layers remaining to be unearthed—since the medium is beside the point when examining the nature of myth. Barthes contends that viewing or understanding an object (raw material) mythically means that the individuality of the object (its place in history) is transformed into that which is perceived as general or universally true: it is identified with "nature." Barthes conflates the layer of the *denoted,* general meaning of myth (the example being the photograph of a black soldier saluting) with "a *perceptual* meaning since it requires a certain training to recognize photo-graphed objects" (Lavers 1980, 110).

In his pieces on photography in *Mythologies,* Barthes assumes a position that perceives the photographic work as a sign capable of being decoded. "Photography and Electoral Appeal" examines the use of photographs as iconographic tokens or symbols used to sell values to an undiscriminating public:

> Photography thus tends to restore the paternalistic nature of elections.
> . . . Inasmuch as photography is an ellipse of language and a condensa-tion of an "ineffable" social whole, it constitutes an anti-intellectual weapon and tends to spirit away "politics" (that is to say a body of problems and solutions) to the advantage of a "manner of being," a socio-moral status. (MY 91)

In a similar vein, the essay "The Great Family of Man" exposes the fact that the "myth of the human 'condition' rests on a very old mystification, which always consists in placing Nature at the bottom of History" (MY 101). Because the exhibition, curated by Edward Steichen and known in English as "The Family of Man," simply presents photographs (and thereby removes history from them), the failure of photography appears flagrant to Barthes: "to reproduce death or birth tells us, literally, nothing" (MY 101). By offering the gestures of man under the alibi of a "wisdom" and a "lyricism," they appear eternal, and their power becomes defused.

"Photos-chocs" is a commentary on an exhibition comprising photo-graphs meant to shock or to surprise. Yet for Barthes the majority of images have no effect, precisely because the photographer has been *too* conscious of how the public will react to his work: "he has almost always *over-constructed* the horror that he propounds, adding to the deed, by contrasts or comminglings, the intentional language of horror" (author's translation). Barthes feels dispossessed of his judgment:

> one has trembled for us, one has reflected for us, one has judged for us; the photographer has left us nothing—only a simple right of intellec-tual acquiescence: we are only drawn to these images by a technical interest; loaded with intervention by the artist himself, they have for us no history, we can no longer *invent* our own response to this synthetic feeding, already perfectly predigested by its creator. (author's translation)

Because the majority of *photos-chocs* chose an intermediary state between the literal deed and the exaggerated deed, they are false: too intentional for the photographer and too exact for the painter. A *photo-choc* succeeds when "that which is *natural* in these images forces the viewer into a violent questioning, the engagement into the path of a judgment that he explores himself without being encumbered by the demiurgic presence of the photographer" (author's translation). Barthes concludes that "literal photography presents the scandal of horror, not the horror itself" (author's translation). Photography is seen as a medium of manipulation in this exhibition, which for the most part leaves Barthes unsatisfied, even piqued, over such intentional engineering of viewer response on the part of the photographer.

It is clear from publications and interviews that by the 1960s Barthes has altered his view concerning semiotics. He no longer sees it as the general science of meaning; instead, he avers: "linguistics *is* the general science of meaning, which can then be subdivided into particular semiotics according to the objects encountered by human language" (GV 65). This statement represents a noteworthy realignment in Barthes's thinking, as it becomes the philosophical starting point for his essays of the 1960s. His concerns rest with articulating the structure of communication in an array of media. Both "The Photographic Message" (1961) and "Rhetoric of the Image" (1964), therefore, center on the construction and conveyance of messages in visual media. The two essays indicate but do not linger on the unique status of the photograph. The photograph holds a privileged relation to literal reality: it is its perfect *analogon*. Beginning with "The Photographic Message," Barthes links this concept to his characterization of the photograph as a message without code in terms of common sense.

From the object to its image, there is of course a reduction: in proportion, in perspective, in color. But this reduction is at no point a *transformation* (in the mathematical sense of the term); to shift from reality to its photograph, it is not at all necessary to break down this reality into units and to constitute these units into signs substantially different from the object they represent; between this object and its image, it is not at all necessary to arrange a relay, i.e., a code; of course, the image is not the reality, but at least it is its perfect *analogon,* and it is just this analogical perfection which, to common sense, defines the photograph. Here appears the particular status of the photographic image: *it is a message without a code;* a proposition from which we must immediately extract an important corollary: the photographic message is a continuous message. (RF 5)

"Of all the structures of information," Barthes postulates, "the photograph is the only one to be exclusively constituted and occupied by a 'denoted' message, which completely exhausts its being" (RF 6). He allows that the purely denotative status of the photograph and the sense of the completeness of its analogy are the characteristics that common sense attributes to the photograph. He even remarks that these commonsense opinions may be mythical. His essay, however, leaves such speculation behind and turns instead to a working hypothesis that "the photographic message (at least the press message) is also connoted" (RF 7). The purpose of the remainder of the essay is to "anticipate the main levels of analysis of photographic connotation" (RF 8). They include trick effects, pose, selection of objects or content, photogenia, aestheticism, and accompanying text. All indicate something about how content, composition, or use can be manipulated, but none provides the basis for understanding the intrinsic difference (if any) between the photograph and any other image.

A "message without code" is logically impossible, at least in terms of Ferdinand de Saussure's semiology, for a "sign" exists strictly because of its position in a coded system. Barthes, however, is using or playing with language and a philosophic construct to convey what was then the unsayable. Film theorists such as Christian Metz, however, drew from the work of American philosopher Charles Sanders Peirce (as well as Saussure) in their articulation of a semiology of the cinema. Peirce had identified three types of signs: (1) *icon,* based on resemblance, a sign that stands for its object essentially by resembling or sharing some of its features; (2) *index,* based on correspondence to fact, a connection to its object by a concrete relationship such as cause and effect; and (3) *symbol,* a general sign that has no natural or resembling connection with its referent. In Peirce's categorization the photograph is an icon. The linguistic paradox, "message without code," is obviated by adopting Peirce's schema.

"Rhetoric of the Image" provides an intriguing glimpse into issues that will fundamentally inform *Camera Lucida,* although the piece remains rooted in concept and tone within the frame of Barthes's structural analyses of the 1960s. Not only does Barthes repeat his statement that the photograph is a "message without code" or "a continuous message," but he also states that "the photograph institutes, in fact, not a consciousness of the thing's *being-*

there (which any copy might provoke), but a consciousness of the thing's *having-been-there*" (RF 33). The sense of "having-been-there" that the photograph invokes for Barthes anticipates significant passages within *Camera Lucida,* but the earlier essay never expands the implications of this quality. The principal argument of this essay is that the rhetoric of the image comprises three messages: linguistic, denoted, and symbolic (cultural or connoted). It is essentially in explicating the denoted message that Barthes must address the inherent difference between a photograph and, for example, a drawing. At the structural level of denotation the photograph presents an "uncoded" message, while the drawing's message subsists as coded. The literal message of the photograph derives not from a transformation between signifieds and signifiers but from a registration that is mechanical. The registration of a drawing, on the other hand, arises through human intervention.

Barthes began "Rhetoric of the Image" with the suggestion that an image's analogical relation to reality represents an inferior meaning and, consequently, claims that he will base his analysis of the image on examples from advertising.

> Why? Because, in advertising, the image's signification is assuredly intentional: it is certain attributes of the product which a priori form the signifieds of the advertising message, and these signifieds must be transmitted as clearly as possible; if the image contains signs, we can be sure that in advertising these signs are replete, formed with a view to the best possible reading: the advertising image is *frank,* or at least emphatic. (RF 22)

In a similar vein, Barthes closes the section entitled "The Denoted Image" by overstepping any development of the complexities of "the photograph as *analogon.*" "The denoted image," he argues, "naturalizes the symbolic message, it makes 'innocent' the very dense (especially in advertising) semantic artifice of connotation" (RF 34). This point is ultimately significant to Barthes because of the danger it portends—the potential use of the photograph to transmute what is, in fact, propaganda into that which seems natural.

> there nonetheless remains in the photograph a kind of natural *being-there* of objects, insofar as the literal message is sufficient: nature seems to produce the represented scene quite spontaneously; the simple

validity of openly semantic systems gives way surreptitiously to a pseudo-truth; the absence of a code deintellectualizes the message because it seems to institute in nature the signs of culture. (RF 34)

In a remark that echoes Walter Benjamin's "The Work of Art in the Age of Mechanical Reproduction," Barthes concludes, "the more technology develops the circulation of information (and notably of images), the more means it provides of masking the constructed meaning under the appearance of the given meaning" (RF 34–35).

Until *Camera Lucida* it can be argued that Barthes retains an allegiance to his statement that the photograph is a message without code or a continuous message. In an interview from 1977 he iterates:

To call photography a language is both true and false. It's false, in the literal sense, because the photographic image is an analogical reproduction of reality, and as such it includes no discontinuous element that could be called *sign:* there is literally no equivalent of a word or letter in a photograph. But the statement is true insofar as the composition and style of a photo function as a secondary message that tells us about the reality depicted and the photographer himself: this is *connotation,* which is language. Photographs always connote something different from what they show on the plane of *denotation.* (GV 353)

Barthes's "recantation" appears in part 2 of *Camera Lucida.* Although he objects to "today's" photographic commentators who reject "reality" in the photograph and maintain that there is nothing but artifice (in other words, codes) at hand, he acknowledges that although nothing can prevent the photograph from being analogical, "at the same time, Photography's *noeme* has nothing to do with analogy (a feature it shares with all kinds of representations). The realists, of whom I am one and of whom I was already one when I asserted that the Photograph was an image without code . . . do not take the photograph for a 'copy' of reality, but for an emanation of *past reality*" (CL 88). This may be viewed as a recantation in the sense that Barthes knows that his essay "The Photographic Message," with its message that the photograph represents an image without code, became a frequent reference or starting point in the subsequent literature on photography; yet he proclaims in the next sentence: "To ask whether a photograph is analogical or coded is not a good means of analysis" (CL 88).

But Barthes has staked his claim regarding this intrinsic difference through his definition of the photographic message as continuous. And once stated, the photograph's continuous message—its message without code—offers little interest to Barthes at this time. If there is no code, there is nothing to analyze, to investigate. Having something to decipher is very important to Barthes. In an interview from 1971, he uses the example of the "happening" to say that everything upon which it is based seems "very dull and impoverished when compared to the values and activities of cheating; I will always defend play against the 'happening.' There is not enough play in the 'happening' because there is no superior game without codes. And so one must take on codes; in order to outplay them, it is necessary to enter into them" (GV 145). This attitude toward codes, even in this seemingly lighthearted context, explains to some extent Barthes's limited exploration of the message without code during the 1960s.

In addition, Barthes's emphasis on language as the source of signification for realia pervades his writings of the 1960s. In *The Fashion System* Barthes does not analyze garments in themselves; his subject matter is what is written about fashion. On the one hand, Barthes indicates that the item under discussion matters little in order to demonstrate his methodology of analyzing meaning through language; and on the other hand, he states that:

> *The Fashion System* can also be understood as a poetic project: the creation of an intellectual object from nothing, or almost nothing. Slowly, before the very eyes of the reader, an intellectual object takes shape in all its complexity. So that one could say . . . : In the beginning, there is nothing, the fashionable garment doesn't exist, it's a thing of great frivolity and no importance . . . but finally a new object comes into existence, created by analysis. (GV 67)

This is Barthes explaining his notion of the creation of myth (myth being a system of communication whereby signification or meaning resides in the language used to discuss or depict a subject): the subject's reality exists through language.

By the 1970s, however, Barthes's critical essays were to undergo a sea change. Most commentators cite *Empire of Signs* (1970) and *S/Z* (1970) as evidence of this shift. One, for example, indicates that "Barthes's disillusionment with semiology after the 1966–70 break coincides with a revised attitude" away from "how a text produces meaning" and toward "meaning" (Ungar 1983, 69). This shift represents a readjustment of focus and not a complete abandonment or denial of the terms, invariably binary, expressed in earlier writings. Barthes's own view of his work is that its source was

> the opacity of social relations, a false Nature; the first impulse, the first shock, then, is to demystify (*Mythologies*); then when the demystification is immobilized in repetition, it must be displaced: semiological *science* (then postulated) tries to stir, to vivify, to arm the mythological gesture, the pose, by endowing it with a method; this science is encumbered in its turn with a whole repertoire of images: the goal of a semiological science is replaced by the (often very grim) science of the semiologists; hence, one must sever oneself from that, must introduce into this rational image-repertoire the texture of desire, the claims of the body: this, then, is the Text, the theory of the Text. But again the Text risks paralysis: it repeats itself, counterfeits itself in lusterless texts, testimonies to a demand for readers, not for a desire to please: the Text tends to degenerate into prattle (*Babil*). Where to go next? That is where I am now. (RB 71)

Barthes's new direction attends to the "signifier" in particular: "I simply wanted to protest . . . in favor of essentially reflexive discourses that initiate, imitate within themselves the infinite nature of language, discourses that never finish up with the demonstration of a signified" (GV 161). Not only has Barthes's semiological methodology depended upon binary oppositions, his approach to all intellectual things has been an acknowledgment and, in fact, a rejoicing in the opposition of values. He equates binarism with eroticism: "everything *with only one difference* produced a kind of joy in him, a continuous astonishment" (RB 52).

Barthes's writings in the 1970s can be characterized as an exploration of the erotic. His subject matter may be the voyager in a foreign (and decidedly exotic) land, such as Japan; or "the eroticism included in the obtuse meaning" (RF 51); or the pleasure (again, the erotic pleasure) of the text; or the discourse of the lover; but he seeks to "know" or examine the signifier and not to provide a merely dogmatic explication of what is signified. He no longer strives to demonstrate that the signified exists; instead, he returns to the source of that which prompts or holds meaning.

This redirection of Barthes's interests does two things. In the first place, it reaffirms the power and pleasure of both reading and writing. It asserts some important oppositions, such as pleasure (*plaisir*) versus bliss (*jouissance,* a term appropriated from Jacques Lacan). Although in the past Barthes has referred to the oppositions of *"plaisir/jouissance," "écriture/écrivance,"* or *"dénotation/connotation"* as voluntarily artificial, he maintains that the difference between the two is quite real. For example:

> Pleasure is linked to a consistence of the self, of the subject, which is assured in values of comfort, relaxation, ease—and for me, that's the entire realm of reading the classics, for example. On the contrary, bliss is the system of reading, or utterance, through which the subject, instead of establishing itself, is lost, experiencing that expenditure which is, properly speaking, bliss. (GV 206)

In the second place, this redirection brings forth a renewed yet somewhat transformed reference to the image. Image is how Barthes now describes his relation to the intertext, the text created by the coming together of the reader's life-text with the author's written text. Barthes offers a description of his view of intertextuality in a 1971 interview with Stephen Heath: "in the intertextual, that is to say, in the texts that surround me, that accompany me, that precede me, that follow me, and with which, of course, I communicate" (author's translation). In explaining his taste for the literature of the past, Barthes uses two arguments:

> first, a metaphor. According to Vico's image, history proceeds in a spiral, and things of the past return, but obviously not in the same place; thus, there are tastes, values, behavior, "writings" of the past that may return, but in a very modern place. The second argument is linked to my work on the amorous subject. This subject develops mainly in a register that, since Lacan, is called *l'imaginaire,* the image-repertoire ...: I have a vital relation to past literature precisely because this literature provides me with images, with a good relation to images. (GV 282–83)

Just as his style of writing became more dependent on the note or the compilation of seemingly fugitive pieces, so too did Barthes's propensity for "fragments, miniatures, partitions, glittering details ..., a bird's-eye view of fields, windows, haiku, line drawing, script, photography, in plays the 'scene' *à l'italienne*" (RB 70) take center stage in his intellectual inquiries. Conversely, in most of his remarks about the cinema, Barthes expresses no passion for this factitious medium, which "excludes by a fatality of Nature all transition to the act: here the image is the *irremediable* absence of the represented body" (RB 84). Not only does the cinema tease the viewer with its illusion of the tangible, but its images fail to provide for or promote pensiveness: their voracity is all-consuming.

Despite Barthes's stated "good relation to images" as proffered by past works of literature, he maintains his long-standing distaste, even hostility, for analogical forms of thought and art. Beginning with his work in *Mythologies*, Barthes has sought to tear asunder the common acceptance that signs are natural:

> I have always been hostile to analogical forms of thought and art. And it's for the opposite reason that I have so loved, if I may say so, the linguistic sign: because I discovered, reading Saussure so many years ago, that there is no analogy within the linguistic sign, that there is no relationship of resemblance between the signifier and the signified. That's something which has always intrigued me in the linguistic sign and in all its transformations into written sentences, texts, and so on.
>
> Further analysis leads us to understand that the denunciation of analogy is in fact a denunciation of the "natural," of pseudo-nature. The social, conformist world always bases its idea of nature on the fact that things resemble each other, and the resulting idea of nature is both artificial and repressive: the "natural," . . . of "what seems natural to most people." (GV 208)

Barthes's antipathy to the analogical and the natural is based on political considerations, that is, "the social, conformist world." In addition, he finds that Lacan's sense of *l'imaginaire* is closely related to "analogy, analogy between images, since the image-repertoire is the register where the subject adheres to an image in a movement of identification that relies in particular on the coalescence of the signifier and the signified" (GV 209). Barthes is conflicted between his abiding disdain for or suspicion of analogy, of which the image seems to partake, and his exploration of *l'imaginaire* as witnessed in his writings of the 1970s. His concern, however, appears to lie not so much with the existence of an image (a stereotype), a myth, or anything that serves as referent or symbol as it does with the public's falling short of recognizing and understanding these images for what they are: tools at the service of manipulators and deceivers. This failure to reflect on or critique (or decode) the world of signs is a lingering complaint for Barthes. Because his writings of the 1970s turn inward to an exploration of self (that is, a methodology described by Barthes in *Camera Lucida* as a *mathesis singularis*), the necessity to rail against the myth ceases.

> So I resolved to start my inquiry with no more than a few photo-graphs, the ones I was sure existed *for me*. Nothing to do with a corpus: only some bodies. In this (after all) conventional debate between science and subjectivity, I had arrived at this curious notion: why mightn't there be, somehow, a new science for each object? A *mathesis singularis* (and no longer *universalis*)? So I decided to take myself as mediator for all Photography. (CL 8).

This reorientation in Barthes's writings releases the image (*l'imaginaire*) and the analogical from the dyspathy expressed in his writings of the 1950s and 1960s. Additionally, Barthes acknowledges in a 1971 article entitled "La mythologie aujourd'hui" that a change had occurred over the past fifteen years in the science of reading: myth, therefore, has become a different object. Now the purpose of the science of the signifier is less the analysis of the sign than its dislocation: it is no longer myths that need to be unmasked; it is the sign itself that must be shaken.

In an interview conducted by Jean Ristat for *Les lettres françaises* (9 February 1972), Barthes is questioned about a science of literature. Barthes admits that he does not believe in scientific discourse, contrary to the conclusion that many seemed to have drawn from *Criticism and Truth*.

> If there is one day a science of literature, it can only be a formal, formalized science: only in that way can it escape the ideological necessity which inhabits all language. I feel there is a scientific image-repertoire, *un imaginaire scientifique*—"*imaginaire*" in the Lacanian sense (a language or set of languages functioning as a misunderstanding of the subject by itself). You have only to read all the social-sciences journals, which are written in a so-called scientific or parascientific style: it would be quite possible to dissect the image-repertoire of these schools. Writing (*écriture*, as opposed to the *écrivance*, the unself-conscious writing of these discourses) is the type of practice that allows us to dissolve the image-repertoires of our language. We make ourselves into psychoanalytical subjects by writing. We conduct a certain type of analysis on ourselves, and at that point the relationship between subject and object is entirely displaced, *invalid*. The old opposition between subjectivity as an attribute of impressionistic criti-

cism and objectivity as an attribute of scientific criticism becomes uninteresting. (GV 164–65)

He expands this critique by stating that the strictly analytical essayist—be (s)he semiologist, structuralist, or whatever—will remain outside reading. "Reading the text" engages one in a manner not consistent with the delineation or verification of structures or narrative models (GV 165). *Ecriture* is an activity in progress, an end unto itself. The writer of *écriture* has read a text on a corporeal, not a conscious level; (s)he has invested the self in the production of said text—the process of how it was written—not the product. These observations figure significantly in Barthes's final excursion on photography, *Camera Lucida*.

Another distinguishing aspect of some of Barthes's writings in the 1970s is his use of photographs or illustrations not simply in the manner of an encyclopedia or reference book—as they primarily functioned in his 1954 book, *Michelet par lui-même*—but as images that conjoin with the texts and inform them. *Empire of Signs* begins with an announcement that "the text does not 'gloss' the images, which do not 'illustrate' the text. . . . Text and image, interlacing, seek to ensure the circulation and exchange of these signifiers: body, face, writing; and in them to read the retreat of signs." The retreat of signs will require a new approach to observation, analysis, and writing on Barthes's part. In *Empire of Signs* several of these changes are attempted at the same time.

In the first place, Barthes challenges himself to locate significance and take on knowledge outside the crucible of the written language of his culture. Japan—a country where "the empire of signifiers is so immense, so in excess of speech, that the exchange of signs remains of a fascinating richness, mobility, and subtlety, despite the opacity of the language" (ES 9)—provides Barthes with a terra incognita for forming a system based on observation alone, without having to deconstruct a preexisting mythology. Conceptually, Barthes's "Japan" is the diametric opposite of the West. The art of Japan, for example, is not mimetic like that of the West, which "struggles to enforce the 'life,' the 'reality' of fictive beings"; rather "the very structure of Japanese restores or confines these beings to their quality as *products,* signs cut off from the alibi referential par excellence: that of the living thing" (ES 7).

Barthes particularly notices this "cutting off" in the Japanese theater, where, for example, "the Oriental transvestite does not copy Woman but signifies her" (ES [53]). What is sought in Japanese theater is not a transfiguration of a specific woman but a translation of femininity to be read, not merely to be seen. European art's dependence on perfecting the illusion of reality is unimportant in Japanese theater and according to Barthes creates a lie (or illusion) that both the actor and the audience struggle to maintain. Barthes contends that the artifice of the Western stage since the Renaissance (its presumption that the audience is spying on the actors onstage) is theological in nature: "it is the space of Sin: on one side, in a light which he pretends to ignore, the actor, i.e., the gesture and the word; on the other, in the darkness, the public, i.e., consciousness" (ES 61). Futile to wonder, he remonstrates, if the audience can ever forget the presence of the manipulators: the metaphorical link that the West establishes between "body and soul, cause and effect, motor and machine, agent and actor, Destiny and man, God and creature" (ES 62) will remain, for the very fact that the manipulators of the Western stage are hidden makes them into a God. Japan has expelled this sort of hysteria from its theater. "In *Bunraku,* the puppet has no strings. No more strings, hence no more metaphor, no more Fate; since the puppet no longer apes the creature, man is no longer a puppet in the divinity's hands, the *inside* no longer commands the *outside*" (ES 62).

The haiku also captivates Barthes. In this art form he confronts "the exemption of meaning." In *Roland Barthes by Roland Barthes* "exemption of meaning" refers to a world of which Barthes dreams, "in which is imagined 'the absence of every sign'" (RB 87). Although Barthes began to write of this dream with *Writing Degree Zero* and continued with a thousand affirmations apropos of the avant-garde text, of Japan, of music, etc., he knows that in public opinion, that is, *Doxa,* there is a curious version of this dream. Having no love of meaning, *Doxa* "counters the invasion of meaning (for which the intellectuals are responsible) by the *concrete;* the concrete is what is supposed to resist meaning" (RB 87). For Barthes the haiku, although intelligible, means nothing. Equally important to Barthes is the fact that haiku never seeks to describe (just as the Japanese theater does not seek to be realistic): its essence is the presentation of a "literally 'untenable' moment in which the thing, though being already only language, will become speech, will pass from one language to another and constitute itself as the memory of this future, thereby anterior"—"[an] apprehension of the thing as event and not as substance" (ES 77–78).

Given the preceding generalities regarding Barthes's view of Japanese art, one can proceed to isolate his metaphorical use of photography in *Empire of Signs.* It includes both the complimentary and the negative. On page 4 of *Empire of Signs* Barthes hastens to claim that in his essay he "has never, in any sense, photographed Japan." He iterates this sentiment five years later in an interview: "I never claimed to be offering a photograph of Japan" (GV 229). Here can be seen Barthes's persistent antipathy to the analogical or realistic (natural) that photography often suggests to him. His antipathy lies with the presumption, so often prevalent, that what the public witnesses is real and without assumptions, without codes, without manipulation. Because Barthes has not yet resolved in his own mind the relation between photography and truth, he vacillates between a fascination for the medium and a loathing for the political or manipulative uses to which it is put and which it often represents to him. In addition, one senses a connotation that photography partakes of the descriptive and/or sterile, both of which are negative qualities absent from the Japanese aesthetic. In a similar vein, the exquisiteness and performance of Japanese cooking are contrasted to the West's "photographed food, the gaudy compositions of our women's magazines" (ES 14). The living quality of the moment that so much of Japanese culture conveys—a quality that relates to a process that Barthes links with writing (écriture)—is initially represented as being at odds with the qualities that Barthes associates with photography.

Satori, a term that may be translated by Westerners as "illumination, revelation, intuition," is defined by Barthes as "no more than a panic suspension of language, the blank which erases in us the reign of the Codes, the breach of that internal recitation which constitutes our person"; a state of "a-language," which is liberating (ES 75). This state is what abolishes the cycle of language that Barthes finds so vicious in Western culture; and he characterizes it as a "flash." At this point in time Barthes's use of the term flash appears to be in contradiction to the flash sometimes associated not only with the photographer's source of light but also with the photograph's ability to capture an instant, a moment in time. Satori means to break forth like a sudden flame, to flare for a moment; photography still connotes darkness and stagnation (camera obscura, not camera lucida or chambre claire).

The mirror is another metaphor commonly associated with photography and one to which Barthes refers in Empire of Signs. "In the West, the mirror is an essentially narcissistic object: man conceives a mirror only in order to look at himself in it; but in the Orient, apparently, the mirror is empty; it is the symbol of the very emptiness of symbols" (ES 78–79). According to one Tao master, "'The mind of the perfect man is like a mirror. It grasps nothing but repulses nothing. It receives but does not retain'" (ES 79). Barthes depicts the Orient's view of the mirror as a device that offers a myriad of reflections, "a repetition without origin." The intangibility connected with the Oriental mirror metaphor and the flash of illumination or perception associated with satori, haiku, and Japanese graphic arts are likened by Barthes to taking a photograph without film.

> Meaning is only a flash, a slash of light: *When the light of sense goes out, but with a flash that has revealed the invisible world,* Shakespeare wrote; but the haiku's flash illumines, reveals nothing; it is the flash of a photograph one takes very carefully (in the Japanese manner) but having neglected to load the camera with film. (ES 83)

Barthes mistakenly attributes the quotation to Shakespeare: it, in fact, derives from William Wordsworth's *Prelude* (Moriarty 1991, 4). The passage, nonetheless, bears witness to the fact that once Barthes makes the association between the photographic sense of flash and of illumination with the Japanese view, he has opened the door to exploring some of the positive qualities that photography evokes.

Another concept that has intrigued Barthes while experiencing his "Japan" is the "trace." Although the "trace" is emphasized by Barthes when discussing the impression left by haiku, it is actually an echo of his discussions regarding the presentation of food in Japan, the nature of much of Japanese graphic art, and even the flavor of finding one's way in Tokyo— "This city can be known only by an activity of an ethnographic kind: you must orient yourself in it not by book, by address, but by walking, by sight, by habit, by experience; here every discovery is intense and fragile, it can be repeated or recovered only by memory of the trace it has left in you" (ES 36). "Trace" (or *trait*) is a "kind of faint gash inscribed upon time, . . . the [privative] 'vision without commentary'" (ES 82).

One of the important qualities invoked by the word *trace* is the sense of a physical presence executed or created in a past time but remaining in present time and possibly to exist in future time. This quality roots the substance/the "thing" in the material or sensual world and not simply in the intellectual world. Beneath a reproduction of a Japanese pen-and-ink or brush-and-ink composition in *Empire of Signs,* Barthes writes: "Where does the writing begin? Where does the painting begin?" (ES [21]). Part of the Japanese aesthetic, Barthes contends, is the value to be had or experienced by the craft or the execution of the final product. The trace of the artist's or writer's hand and the commingling of media traditionally kept separate in the West create an awareness, even a sensual joy, in the fluidity of life. The recognition of the importance of the physical trace allows the physicality of the photograph—the uniqueness that distinguishes the photograph—to come center stage. Although this appearance will not take place until *Camera Lucida,* it is prefigured in *Empire of Signs* in general and in particular when Barthes draws the reader's attention to photographs of General Nogi and of his wife.

Barthes becomes very specific regarding these photographs. He tells the reader that they were taken on 13 September 1912; that General Nogi was victor over the Russians at Port Arthur; that the Emperor of Japan has "just" died; that the General and his wife "have decided to commit suicide the following day" (ES 91). One is looking at faces that know precisely when they are going to die. Although Barthes's point is that these photographic portraits represent or indicate the exemption of death's meaning, he can draw that conclusion only because the portraits are photographs, more particularly, photographs rooted in a precise time and place. He, in 1970, is able to partake of the living experience of those outside of his time and place, because their physical trace remains to be confronted or examined.

In Japan the frame or fragment is more important, more meaningful than the whole.

It is no longer the great continuous wall which defines space, but the very abstraction of the fragments of view (of the "views") which frame me; the wall is destroyed beneath the inscription; the garden is a mineral tapestry of tiny volumes (stones, traces of the rake on the sand), the public place is a series of instantaneous events which accede to the notable in a flash so vivid, so tenuous that the sign does away with itself before any particular signified has had the time to "take." (ES 107–8)

So at least in Japan, Barthes can find purpose in considering the photographic portraits of General Nogi and his wife, for there is no separation between the individual and his or her physical or public presentation: a momentary rendering conveys his or her essence and "accede[s] to the notable in a flash." "Michelet, l'Histoire et la Mort" (1952) contains one of Barthes's earliest images of photography: "Thus the flesh of men who follow each other preserves the obscure trace of the incidents of History, until the day when the historian, like a photographer, *reveals* through a chemical operation that which has previously been experienced" (quoted in Lombardo 1989, 139). The quotation confirms the association that Barthes sees between the trace and the activity or essence of photography.

Barthes begins *Empire of Signs* asserting that he has in no way "photographed" Japan. In continuation, he claims that "he has done the opposite: Japan has starred him with any number of 'flashes'" (ES 4). What Barthes does not consider at the outset nor completely reconcile within this text is the power of the photograph to transcend his own negative myths and, in fact, represent or partake of the "frame," the "trace," and the "flash" that characterize the pleasure and excitement that he discovered in Japan. Yet the passage in thought to which *Empire of Signs* attests is a vital one for Barthes's intellectual journey concerning photography, for it introduces a new perspective on his consideration of the image and—like another piece of writing from 1970—explores with greater clarity the concept of the "exemption of meaning."

In another work of 1970 Barthes offers some thoughts on the filmmaker Sergei Eisenstein. The focus of Barthes's essay "The Third Meaning" is not the moving pictures that Eisenstein has created but rather the movie stills that have accompanied his works. The first two meanings that Barthes ascribes to the photographic still are (1) informational, which serves the realm of communication, and (2) symbolic, which functions on at least four levels—referential, diegetic, Eisensteinian, and historical—and which represents the still's signification. Yet to such seemingly complete categories with regard to "meaning" in the photograph, Barthes feels compelled to add a third, for, quite simply, the first and second meanings are obvious. In relation to the second meaning Barthes writes: "The symbolic meaning . . . is intentional (it is what the author has meant) and it is selected from a kind of general, common lexicon of symbols; it is a meaning which seeks me out—me, the recipient of the message, the subject of the reading—a meaning which proceeds from Eisenstein and moves *ahead of me*" (RF 43–44). The meaning is evident in "a *closed* sense": "the obvious meaning is the one 'which presents itself quite naturally to the mind'" (RF 44).

To the stratification and understanding of meaning Barthes inserts the proposition that something may remain in the analysis of the photographic still that "transcends" conventional or obvious meaning, something that he cannot be "certain . . . is justified—if it can be generalized" (RF 43). The third meaning "possesses a theoretical individuality"; its realm is that of "*signifying* [*signifiance*], a word that has the advantage of referring to the field of the signifier (and not of signification) and of approaching, along the trail blazed by Julia Kristeva, who proposed the term, a semiotics of the text" (RF 43). Barthes distinguishes this meaning as obtuse, that "which appears 'in excess,' as a supplement my intellection cannot quite absorb, a meaning both persistent and fugitive, apparent and evasive" (RF 44). And in a refrain that will appear ten years later in *Camera Lucida,* Barthes speaks of the obtuse meaning extending "beyond culture, knowledge, information" (RF 44).

In the Eisenstein stills Barthes believes that he recognizes something that was not intentional to Eisenstein—something that "carries a certain *emotion* . . . [that] is never viscous; it is an emotion which simply *designates* what is loved, what is to be defended; it is an emotion-as-value" (RF 51). Within the actor's disguise Barthes sees an excess that concomitantly mocks the expression of feeling or emotion while maintaining the dignity or power of that emotion. "The obtuse meaning is not in the language system (even that of symbols)" (RF 51, 54). Barthes's ability to discuss the obtuse meaning is thwarted by description and by analysis. As he explains, he can merely designate a site in which he senses an obtuse meaning: he can point but not transcribe—nor would there be any value for him to attempt to transform, for it is a "signifier without signified" (RF 55).

With regard to the development of Barthes's views on photography, *Empire of Signs* releases a complicated new agenda for appreciating the visual, while "The Third Meaning" unwittingly (so it seems) introduces the notion of the miraculous that a given movie still may contain or have the presence to convey. It is unwitting in the sense that Barthes does not emphasize the obtuse meaning as being unique to the photograph. Given the context of the photographs discussed, Barthes's thread of inquiry appears to fall within a discussion of the intentionality of an artist and the points that lay outside this intentionality yet, nonetheless, register meaning. Using the terminology of the cinema, Barthes says that "the obtuse meaning is clearly the epitome of counter-narrative; disseminated, reversible, trapped in its own temporality, it can establish (if followed) only an altogether different 'script' from the one of shots, sequences, and syntagms (whether technical or narrative): an unheard-of script, counter-logical and yet 'true'" (RF 57). For Barthes the third meaning in the film is the "filmic," and it is akin to the "novelistic" in the novel. It's a *je ne sais quoi* that transcends yet remains allied to whatever medium is being considered. Profoundly, the obtuse meaning copies nothing, represents nothing. And as Barthes will come to write more dramatically or fatalistically in *Camera Lucida,* "it is precisely in this *arrest* of interpretation that the Photograph's certainty resides. . . . But also, unfortunately, it is in proportion to its certainty that I can say nothing about this photograph" (CL 107).

The essay "The Third Meaning" clearly puts forth the concept that there remains "meaning" that the metalanguage of criticism cannot capture. In its dissociation from the text (text being any medium or genre), the third or obtuse meaning distances itself from not only the narrative of the medium itself but also the narrative of analysis and criticism. Barthes paradoxically indicates that although semantically he must locate the obtuse outside of language and outside of the structure of the medium, it nevertheless is linked to that medium. So the movie still is perceived not so much as an example of the medium of photography as it is an extract of the medium of film. He even suggests that the obtuse meaning can be shared.

> Consequently, if we remain, you and I, on the level of articulated language in the presence of these images—that is, on the level of my own text—the obtuse meaning will not come into being, will not enter into the critic's metalanguage. Which means that the obtuse meaning is outside (articulated) language, but still within interlocution. For if you look at these images I am talking about, you will see the meaning: we can understand each other about it "over the shoulder" or "on the back" of articulated language: thanks to the image (frozen, it is true: I shall return to this), indeed thanks to what in the image is purely image (and which, to tell the truth, is very little indeed), we do without speech yet continue to understand each other. (RF 55)

Barthes associates—rightly so—the still photographs with the moving pictures that they represent. His analysis, therefore, of the nature of the obtuse meaning resides in an artifact that derives its existence from a text—the narrative of the cinema. Even though the still may transcend that text and the metalanguage of the critic, its context remains that of the cinematic genre.

In the concluding section of "The Third Meaning," which is entitled "The Still," Barthes assumes for the movie still its exclusive ability to conjoin a third meaning. "Neither the simple photograph nor the figurative painting can assume," states Barthes, "[a third meaning] because they lack the diegetic horizon, the possibility of configuration" (that is, "a mutation which can lead to a complete reversal of values") (RF 60). As significant as Barthes's articulation and analysis of the obtuse meaning is both in this initial essay and in the resonances within his writings of the 1970s, nothing is acknowledged that is intrinsic to the medium of photography per se. Yet when Barthes does refocus on the medium of photography in *Camera Lucida,* the movie still that "gives us the *inside* of the fragment" can now be compared with the potential of all photographs (not just movie stills) to punctuate history, to be "the fragment of a second text *whose existence never exceeds the fragment*" (RF 61).

Barthes considers the time of cinema a constraint—a constraint to lingering, a constraint to seeing or noticing, and, ultimately, a constraint to understanding and appreciating. Movement, therefore, is something that he is loathe to acknowledge as the essence of film: it functions, he asserts, much like the plot of a novel, "merely the armature of a permutational unfolding" (RF 61). "The still, by instituting a reading which is at once instantaneous and vertical, flouts logical time (which is only an operational time)" (RF 62). Barthes concludes by recognizing that what he is truly seeking is "an authentic mutation of reading and its object, text or film" (RF 62). So the essay ends in closer alignment to his considerations of the writerly and readerly texts in *S/Z* than with any previous or subsequent discussions on photography.

By 1975 and the publication of *Roland Barthes by Roland Barthes*, images in general are simply joyous to Barthes and the photographic image predominates. The text of *Roland Barthes* repeats many of the considerations and conclusions found in *Empire of Signs* and "The Third Meaning" but also adds or reinforces a few additional concepts that are significant to photography. *Gesture* is a recurring notion in Barthes's work, particularly that of the 1970s. Its cultural antecedent for Barthes is Baudelaire.

Predilection for Baudelaire's phrase, quoted several times (notably apropos of wrestling matches): "the emphatic truth of gesture in the great circumstances of life." He [Barthes] called this excess of pose the *numen* (which is the silent gesture of the gods pronouncing on human fate). The *numen* is hysteria frozen, eternalized, trapped, since it is at last held motionless, pinioned by a long stare. Whence my interest in poses (provided they are framed), noble paintings, pathetic scenes, eyes raised to heaven, etc. (RB 134)

Barthes is a step away from acknowledging part of the power and fascination of photography's potential: a potential that he does examine in *Camera Lucida*. As in the art criticism of Baudelaire, the relationship between the gesture and photography is not immediately made yet conceptually cannot be denied.

Stéphane Mallarmé also speaks of gestures: "gestures of ideas." According to Barthes, Mallarmé "finds the gesture first (expression of the body), then the idea (expression of the culture, of the intertext)" (RB 99). So, too, asserts Barthes, does he: "philosophy then is no more than a reservoir of particular images, of ideal fictions (he borrows objects, not reasonings)" (RB 99). Barthes does not start with an idea for which he then invents an image: such an approach is precisely what he has spent over twenty years debunking. Instead, the sensuous object may lead him toward "an *abstraction* for it, levied on the intellectual culture of the moment" (RB 99). He wants to know or experience the object for itself and not simply for the ideology that it serves.

Barthes struggles to reconcile "meaning" as it appears in public opinion with something else that has no name. "It is not a question of recovering a pre-meaning, . . . but rather to imagine a post-meaning: one must traverse, as though the length of an initiatic way, the whole meaning, in order to be able to extenuate it, to exempt it" (RB 87). He senses a contradiction or irony between *Doxa,* public or common opinion, which also has no love for meaning, and his own dream of a world "exempt of meaning." "Whence a double tactic: against *Doxa,* one must come out in favor of meaning, for meaning is the product of History, not of Nature; but against Science (paranoiac discourse), one must maintain the utopia of suppressed meaning" (RB 87).

Barthes frequently refers to images and objects that allow him to "maintain the utopia of suppressed meaning" as "mat": a surface or quality that does not offer one's own image back but absorbs one into itself, as does the Japanese sense of "mirror." The concept of the fragment remains torn for Barthes between the public's tendency to draw meaning or a lesson from each fragment of life and the converse (Barthes's ideal), which is to take "incidents" of life and "refuse ever to draw a line of meaning from them" (RB 151). "Mat" evinces the sense of "in-significance" from which Barthes ultimately derives a *significance* allied to enchantment.

Enchantment, fascination, enthrallment—all conjure a sense of magic or sorcery that vitiates logical explication and universal agreement. The collection of images that opens *Roland Barthes* attests to this quality of pleasure, which eludes descriptive, psychological, or philosophic reasonings.

> *To begin with, some images: they are the author's treat to himself, for finishing his book. His pleasure is a matter of fascination (and thereby quite selfish). I have kept only the images which enthrall me,* without my knowing why *(such ignorance is the very nature of fascination, and what I shall say about each image will never be anything but . . . imaginary).* (RB [3])

The thirty-nine photographs, one lithograph, and three manuscripts that comprise the first quarter of the text form a repertoire for Barthes's existence before his self-awareness of writing. On the one hand, these images spark memories (not, however, nostalgic memories) of his young life and its environs, and by *studium* he takes his interest in them. On the other hand, some of these images captivate him because of their *punctum,* that is, the housemaid who "fascinates" Barthes: she stands in shadow in a doorway in the background and to the side in a photograph of Barthes's grandmother (RB [13]). From time to time Barthes's sense of physical loss is juxtaposed with the photograph as surviving record of or testament to the object's onetime existence: *"(The house is gone now, swept away by the housing projects of Bayonne)"* (RB [8]). Barthes also refers to the photograph as record of lineage—the family album that traces the ties of flesh and blood outlined in faces, in limbs, in postures, and in expressions. *"The family novel. Where do they come from? From a family of notaries in the Haute-Garonne. Thereby endowing me with a race, a class. As the (official) photograph proves"* (RB [19]). And finally, images, particularly photographs, connote the mirror and also the lens: devices that distance Barthes from himself. *"You are the only one who can never see yourself except as an image; you never see your eyes unless they are dulled by the gaze they rest upon the mirror or the lens"* (RB [36]).

An image, a scene, or a moment in time can pierce Barthes and convey an essence or a reality too overwhelming to be denied. "Le hasard" can produce "that rare moment in which the whole *symbolic* accumulates and forces the body to yield . . . [to] the very *being* of exclusion" (RB 86). "*Detached:* forever assigned the place of the *witness*" (RB 86), Barthes acknowledges that he is not a maker of or a participant in images. His relation to them, therefore, will remain "subject to codes of detachment: either narrative, or explicative, or challenging, or ironic: never *lyrical,* never homogenous with the pathos outside of which he must seek his place" (RB 86).

In 1978 Barthes wrote a brief essay for an Italian publication concerning the photographs of Baron Wilhelm von Gloeden; it was reprinted in *L'obvie et l'obtus: Essais Critiques III* (1982). This work presents Barthes extolling the medium of photography for its paradoxical qualities. The Baron's engagement of local boys as photographic models provides a strange mix of subjects (the dark-skinned Italian peasants) with subject matter ("a Greek version of antiquity"). Similarly, Barthes is fascinated by the contradiction of photography as reputed to be "an exact, empirical art entirely in the service of such positive, rational values as authenticity, reality, objectivity" (RF 196) and its use in von Gloeden's artistic vision. "This carnival of contradictions," which his work conveys, is "why von Gloeden's art is such an adventure of meaning" and remains "a counter-oneirism crazier than the craziest dreams" (RF 196–97).

It is important to lay bare the twists of meaning that Barthes attributes to the photograph, once the analysis of connoted messages or codes subsides as Barthes's primary interest. Also important is the recognition that Barthes consciously refrains from drawing comprehensive conclusions regarding the medium in *Roland Barthes,* while openly acknowledging his positive response to the medium's use in his von Gloeden introduction. The impulse conveyed in "The Photographic Message" to situate photography's *noeme* in the notion of a message without code conflicts with the impulse clearly at hand in *Empire of Signs* to consider the photograph as disrupter in time's linear flow (for example, the photographs of General Nogi and wife); the impulse implied in "The Third Meaning" that the photograph may contain more than that which is intended by the artist; the impulse in *Roland Barthes* to present a multidimensional view of the photograph's essence; and the impulse in "Baron von Gloeden" to flirt with the madness of photography. Barthes's original paradox vis-à-vis the photograph—its continuous message—has already been replaced in the von Gloeden introduction by a paradox concerning the real, authenticity, and art. In *Camera Lucida* the photographic paradox will be refined to one involving time. This transformation emerges from a maze of paths presented in the now-familiar Barthesian style of the fragment: the dispersion of "the notes or reflections on photography within a system of writing that undermines definitive interpretation," amounting to a "strategy of interruption" (Ungar 1983, 154). And this transformation is had at the expense of focusing on the photographer, for as Wright Morris states, the mythical power of the medium emerges only as the hand of the photographer recedes.

2. Mythologies of the Photograph

> We *regard* the photograph, the picture on our wall, as the object itself (the man, landscape, and so on) depicted there.
>   This need not have been so. We could easily imagine people who did not have this relation to such pictures. Who, for example, would be repelled by photographs, because a face without colour and even perhaps a face in reduced proportions struck them as inhuman.
>
>   Ludwig Wittgenstein, *Philosophical Investigations*

Mythologies—originally published in 1957, reissued in 1970, and translated into English in 1972—challenges the reader to investigate the "ideological abuse" hidden in "the decorative display of *what-goes-without saying*" (MY 11). In the preface to the 1970 edition Barthes acknowledges that the execution of his original objective appears too naive for today's sophisticated and complex analyses and methodologies. Yet in *Camera Lucida* it may be argued that the stance Barthes takes on photography itself begins in mythology. This positioning within certain myths of the photograph is self-conscious on Barthes's part; it represents the intertextual display of what-goes-without saying devoid of any determination toward ideological abuse.

Even Barthes's essays on photography from the 1960s exhibit a mythological base. The myth of the photograph, for example, that he brings to his essay "The Photographic Message" is its "denotative status." Barthes maintains that photography does not transform reality but is, in fact, its *analogon*. He contends that, except for photographs, in all analogical reproductions of reality, from drawings and paintings to movies and theatrical performances, the style of the reproduction—its "treatment" by the creator—overwhelms the attempt to achieve that very realism. In contradistinction, in the photograph what we first "see," according to Barthes, is literal reality. He presents this point by referencing the rhetoric of one of Western photography's two predominant myths: in the press photograph, Barthes notes, what is at service is an image that offers itself "as a mechanical analogue of reality"

(RF 6).The signifying term is "mechanical." In order to draw his differentia-
tion between photographs and all other realistic visual media, Barthes relies
on the positivistic myth that if the document or testimony is mechanical—
or if it partakes of the mechanical—then subjectivity is eliminated or
reduced. In "The Photographic Message" Barthes marginalizes the mythological aspects of this statement: he refers to the photograph's apparent
objectivity or perception of objectivity as *risking* being mythical and paren-
thetically notes that these characteristics are attributed to the photograph by
common sense. Toward the end of the essay, however, Barthes returns to the
myth of the photograph as testimony. In discussing "strictly traumatic
images," he perceives that as trauma "is just what suspends language and
blocks signification," so too does the photograph's denotative status essentially impede the messaging of connotation. "We might imagine a kind of
law: the more direct the trauma, the more difficult the connotation; or even:
the 'mythological' effect of a photograph is inversely proportional to its
traumatic effect" (RF 19–20). Barthes associates the "mechanical" photograph as being without culture and sees the photographic paradox as that
which "makes an inert object into a language and which transforms the
non-culture of a 'mechanical' art into the most social of institutions" (RF
20). Yet it can be construed that a more puzzling paradox resides in the
linkage of the phenomenon of photography—in its essence—to non-culture. Barthes will revisit and invert the notion in *Camera Lucida* when he
proposes that he wants "to be a primitive, without culture" when "looking
at certain photographs" (CL 7).

"Rhetoric of the Image" establishes its tripartite system of messages on
the proposition that both photographic and drawn or painted images used in
advertising possess a literal or denoted message. It begins, in fact, with the
equivalent of the maxim "Seeing is believing." Within the first paragraph
Barthes asserts: "public opinion . . . vaguely regards the image as a site of
resistance to meaning, in the name of a certain mythical notion of Life: the
image is re-presentation, i.e., ultimately resurrection" (RF 21). The photograph, however, achieves literal presentation by its very essence, while the
drawing or painting can never convey "a literal image in the pure state" (RF
31). When Barthes proceeds to discuss the denoted image, difficulties arise.
Earlier in the essay he had already repeated his position that photographic
signifiers are *not* arbitrary (as they are in speech)—the paradox of a message
without code. In order, however, to articulate the "denoted" message, he
resorts to words such as "utopian," "pure," and "absolutely" to form a base of
comparison not only between photographs and all other images (in advertis-

ing) but also between the appearance of "naturalness" in images and the possible manipulation of that appearance. As he did at the end of "The Photographic Message," Barthes links the "pure" imagery of the photograph to nonculture, while maintaining that the visual messaging of a drawing, for example, can never elide culture. What seems problematic in his position—although he remains quite consistent with his earlier essay—is the lack of exploration of how something like the medium of photography can be outside culture. Although Barthes alludes to the transfiguration—as opposed to the transformation—of the visual by photography, he still fails to investigate more carefully whether or not his stance toward the medium is itself mythical. Given his renown in discussing and analyzing cultural mythologies, Barthes's disinterest at this time in wrestling with the myths surrounding photography in the Western world is noteworthy.

At the heart of *Camera Lucida* lie certain mythological suppositions that history not only records but also empowers. In an interview from 1980 Barthes explains that the work is

> like a phenomenology of photography. I consider the phenomenon of photography in its absolute novelty in world history. The world has existed for hundreds of thousands of years, there have been images for thousands of years, since the cave paintings. . . . There are millions of images in the world. And then, all at once, around 1822, a new type of image appears, a new iconic phenomenon, entirely, anthropologically new.
>
> It's this newness that I try to examine, and I place myself in the situation of a naïve man, outside culture, someone untutored who would be constantly astonished at photography. (GV 357)

This is a provocative proposition whose simplicity of statement belies its philosophical complexity. Barthes's position in *Camera Lucida* needs to be evaluated in relation to the history of Western photography as he is likely to have understood it, but it also needs to be analyzed in terms of the proposition itself—that one can stand "outside culture." As John Berger has noted, the beginnings of photography inform our views of the medium today. He remarks that "the decline of religion corresponds with the rise of the photograph" (Berger 1980, 53) and suggests that as democracy and science supplanted religion in the nineteenth century, photography "for a brief moment . . . was considered to be an aid to these agents" (Berger 1980, 54). His conclusion is unequivocal: "It is still to this historical moment that photography owes its ethical reputation as Truth" (Berger 1980, 54). Precisely because the initial conceptions and metaphorical descriptions of photography adhere (in varying degrees) to today's conceptions of and metaphors about photography, they offer insight into Barthes's writings on photography. Barthes not only indicates that he has surveyed a general assortment of histories of photography before embarking on his essay, he cites historical facts and trivia throughout the book.

The first paragraph of *Camera Lucida* invokes the realm of history with the concomitant yet contradictory qualities of connection and separation. Here Barthes expresses his amazement that when looking at a photograph of Napoleon's younger brother Barthes is "looking at eyes that looked at the Emperor." He points out that his amazement was not generally shared: "Life consists of these little touches of solitude" (CL 3). A similar sense of isolation informs *Quand j'étais photographe* (1900), the memoir of the famed nineteenth-century Parisian photographer Nadar. He strives to recapture the newness, the marvel of this invention in a time when "this mystery" had been converted to the "commonplace" (Krauss 1982, 118–19). Nadar's memoir reveals a mind still astonished at the importance of photography as a scientific invention rivaling "the steam engine, the electric light, the telephone, the phonograph, the radio, bacteriology, anesthesiology, psychophysiology" (Krauss 1982, 118). But Nadar also invokes one of the other compelling myths associated with photography—the perception that the physical referent is photography's "absolute requirement," for "photography depends on an act of passage between two bodies in the same space. . . . Nadar circles around what seems for him to be the central fact of photography: that its operation is that of the imprint, the register, the trace" (Krauss 1982, 121).

The sense of the photograph as imprint comes to life in Nadar's memoir when recalling Honoré de Balzac, whose daguerreotype portrait Nadar had purchased from the artist Gavarni. Nadar claims that Balzac had a fear or horror of photography because he believed that a "ghostly" layer of his own self was being removed when his photograph was *taken*. Nadar's recollection of Balzac may have been informed by Balzac's own writing in his novel *Cousin Pons.* In one of the narrator's excursions into philosophy and commentary on contemporary society, daguerreotypy is, in fact, referred to as an invention that proves or acknowledges that "a building or a figure is at all times and in all places represented by an image in the atmosphere, that every existing object has a spectral intangible double which may become visible" (Balzac 1971, 112–13). The narrator then returns to his discussion of occult science and argues for the consideration of the coexistence of past, present, and future time.

> Remark that it is not really more wonderful that the seer should foretell the chief events of the future than he should read the past. Past and future, on the skeptic's system, equally lie beyond the limits of knowledge. If the past has left traces behind it, it is not improbable that future events have, as it were, their roots in the present.
>
> If a fortune-teller gives you minute details of past facts known only to yourself, why should he not foresee the events to be produced by existing causes? The world of ideas is cut out, so to speak, on the pattern of the physical world; the same phenomena should be discernible in both, allowing for the difference in the medium. As, for instance, a corporeal body actually projects an image upon the atmosphere—a spectral double detected and recorded by the daguerreotype. (Balzac 1971, 114–15)

Nadar's sense of marvel and Balzac's sense of spiritism regarding photography function as signifying intertexts for *Camera Lucida*. Their nineteenth-century sensibilities serve as a starting point in *Camera Lucida* for Barthes's examination of photography today. At one point he likens the photograph to "a skin I share with anyone who has been photographed" (CL 81). This carnal medium acts as "a sort of umbilical cord [that] links the body of the photographed thing to my gaze" (CL 81). Barthes's insistence that he approach his study with naïveté may, in fact, confound prevailing theoretical stances: "Barthes boldly assumes a naïveté of regard, of consciousness, that the more or less successive theories—Marxist, Freudian, linguistic, sociological—seemed to have condemned" (Rabaté 1986, 29; author's translation).

Balzac's view of daguerreotypy represents only one of the ways that photography astonishes the naive man. Historically, photography is the product of two predominant impulses: one being the effort to fix the image of the camera obscura, the other being the struggle to control and ultimately to halt the chemical reactions set in motion when light is brought to bear on certain substances such as silver salts. The former concern describes the early photographic experimenters in England, for example, Thomas Wedgwood, Sir Humphrey Davy, and William Henry Fox Talbot. The latter bespeaks the experimenters in France, such as Joseph Nicéphore Niépce (considered to be the first to produce a photograph) and Louis Jacques Mandé Daguerre. In a quirk of fate practical photography was discovered independently by two men in two different countries (Daguerre in France and Talbot in England), and both revealed their work to the public in the same year, 1839.

When Wittgenstein suggests that one could imagine people repelled by photographs in which the human face appears without color and in reduced proportions, he is formulating a philosophical argument that relates to the proposition that the only necessity is logical necessity. His suggestion that a different reaction to photography is logically possible is ahistorical. In terms of Western culture, however, there was an enormous likelihood for the reaction that Wittgenstein first states—"we *regard* the photograph . . . as the object itself"—because the invention was a by-product or culmination of nearly twenty-three centuries of fascination with and knowledge of the principles of the camera obscura. Since the time of Aristotle, the principles of the camera obscura have been known. The device itself, from which the photographic camera directly descends, was in regular use in the Arab world by the eleventh century and was commonplace to scholars in western Europe by the fifteenth century. The private manuscripts of Leonardo da Vinci reveal his complete knowledge of and familiarity with the mechanism. The earliest published account of the camera obscura is found in an annotation in the first Italian edition (1521) of Vitruvius's *Treatise on Architecture* (Gernsheim 1982). By the middle of the sixteenth century Giovanni Battista della Porta's recommendation that the camera obscura could assist artists in their drawing was becoming widely accepted in the Western world.

Since the sixteenth century, therefore, proportion was a hallmark of Western art. According to Barthes this line of inquiry does not concern him, for he associates the camera obscura with the photographer, the "Operator."

> I might suppose that the *Operator's* emotion (and consequently the essence of Photography-according-to-the-Photographer) had some relation to the "little hole" (*stenope*) through which he looks, limits, frames, and perspectivizes when he wants to "take" (to surprise). . . . The *Operator's* Photograph . . . was linked to the vision framed by the keyhole of the *camera obscura*. (CL 9–10)

Barthes observes two other categories for the photograph: "to undergo" (*subir*), which is related to the "*Spectrum*"—"the person or thing photographed is the target, the referent, a kind of little simulacrum, any *eidolon* emitted by the object, which I should like to call the *Spectrum* of the

Photograph" (CL 9)—and "to look" (*regarder*), which is related to the "*Spectator*"—"The *Spectator* is ourselves, all of us who glance through collections of photographs—in magazines and newspapers, in books, albums, archives" (CL 9). According to Barthes the latter category partakes of the chemical order of photography: "It seemed to me that the *Spectator's* Photograph descended essentially, so to speak, from the chemical revelation of the object (from which I receive, by deferred action, the rays)" (CL 10).

As early as the time of the ancient Greeks the effect of light action had been noted (Eder 1945). Alchemists were also aware of the importance and power of light.

> The alchemists . . . had only hazy, mystic conceptions of the influence of the all-animating sun and of astrology on the successful working out of the chemical processes by which they endeavored to change base metals into gold and silver. Nevertheless, their ideas were the starting point for a number of chemical experiments, which led to the discovery of phosphorescent bodies in the seventeenth and eighteenth centuries and to the discovery of the light sensitiveness of the silver salts. (Eder 1945, 21)

The history of chemistry as it relates to photography ranges from an eighth-century Arabian alchemist producing nitrate of silver by dissolving silver in nitric acid; to Georg Fabricius discovering in 1565 that chloride of silver exists as a mineral in nature; to the seventeenth-century scientists Angelo Sala and Wilhelm Homberg, who independently attributed the darkening of silver salts to the sun; to Johann Heinrich Schulze, professor of anatomy at the University of Altdorf near Nuremberg. To the latter goes the distinction of recognizing and proving that the action of light—and not the action of heat—is responsible for the darkening of silver salts. As early as 1729 Schulze was applying his knowledge to "inscribe, or copy ('inscribere'), written characters by the aid of light" (Eder 1945, 62). (Although this discovery was of monumental significance to subsequent photographic experimenters, Schulze's work did not extend to attempting to arrest and make permanent the light-induced chemical reaction.) Niépce's photographic experiments derived from his work in lithography and began with heliography or sun drawing (as opposed to trying to project and then fix the image projected through a peephole). His work was joined with and ultimately completed by that of Daguerre. Photography's chemical lineage, therefore, provides a rich mythological or symbolic field for Barthes—an alternative to the perceived limits or clichés gleaned from the rhetoric of the camera obscura. The chemical order suggests alchemy with its sense of magic and the quasi-mystical notion of transmutation by means of light (the all-animating sun).

This "prehistory" of photography suffices to articulate the binary opposition that Barthes erects in part 1 of *Camera Lucida* between the camera box with its pinhole or lens and the chemicals touched by light rays. Yet he also contends that he is approaching his analysis of photography "outside culture." According to an interview conducted by Guy Mandery in December 1979, Barthes considers the golden age of photography to be its beginnings and refers to this time as "its heroic period" (GV 359). Yet in another interview published in *Le Matin,* 22 February 1980, he indicates disdain for the University of Aix-Marseille for placing an ad hoc photography center in the chemistry department: "as if photography were still dependent on its heroic beginnings, as far as the university is concerned" (GV 351). Yet it is to the *chemical order* of photography that Barthes is drawn in *Camera Lucida.*

Barthes appears conflicted between his intention to consider photography "outside culture" with "naïveté" and his affinity to his own cultural past. His statement that the chemical discovery was perhaps the essential one among the causes of photography (CL 31) is not simply a technical or scientific one. By aligning himself with the notion of photography as magic, he manifests a sensibility uncommon in his own time yet compelling in the first decade or so of photography's public existence (and to a lesser extent throughout the nineteenth century). And this sensibility bespeaks Daguerre, not Talbot. Even at its birth and in its youth photography suggested different things to different people; from initial reactions to the medium, two dominant mythologies emerged.

As cultural icons, Talbot and Daguerre represent two distinct ways of viewing photography, as well as two differing ways of "locating" its origins. Talbot partakes of a scientific, progressive view of the development of human potential and achievement. As a "gentleman" classicist, mathematician, and inventor, he worked slowly and systematically to "cause these natural images" ("which the glass lens of the Camera [obscura] throws upon the paper in focus") "to imprint themselves durably, and remain fixed upon the paper!" (Talbot [1844, 1846] 1969). As an amateur scientist in Victorian England, Talbot sought and promoted the practical applications of his photographic invention, while at the same time giving proper Victorian consideration to the pleasing arrangement of subject matter within his photographic compositions.

Talbot's own remarks about his photographic work convey a sense of delight in the permanent rendering of nature's "fairy pictures, creations of the moment"; a sense of pride in and excitement over humankind's progress and his part in it; but ultimately a sense of bitterness that Daguerre and the daguerreotype were more popular and more acclaimed than Talbot and the Talbotype. Simply put, Talbot and the initial samples of his work did not capture the world's imagination. This failure to ignite the *popular* imagination of his time ultimately relates to aesthetics. Although one of the obstacles to the widespread use of Talbot's technique was the patent that he insisted on taking out and enforcing on his process, his technique, nonetheless, did not produce the visual novelty of the daguerreotype and was judged accordingly. Calotypes, later renamed Talbotypes by Talbot, were photographic prints produced on paper through the medium of a paper negative, thus lacking the visual clarity and sharpness of detail that typified the daguerreotype. Today Talbot's concept of a negative/positive process is the norm, but the result in 1839 and the 1840s was an object extraordinarily reminiscent of an etching or lithograph, even perhaps a pencil drawing. Visually, the Talbotype did not appear substantially new or different, although the method of creating a Talbotype was revolutionary. Talbot was so worried that the public might not realize that the plates in *The Pencil of Nature* were photographs that he explicitly states in his introductory remarks that the reader should be aware that his new art of photogenic drawing and the ensuing examples are not the results of any artist or engraver.

Talbot supported the alliance of science and art: the improvement of art by science and the sophistication of science by art. He looked for "fundamental components, [the] 'ultimate nature' [of things] in order to perceive clearly the natural world and man's place within it" (Buckland 1980, 13). In contrast, Daguerre represents the world of art, of illusion, of perfection of detail, and of entertainment for the general public. Initially a stage designer with a specialty for lighting effects and trompe l'oeil graphic displays, Daguerre became so successful, so acclaimed that the critics as well as the public would attend plays considered not worth viewing simply because they valued Daguerre's work. "He understood better than anyone else how to vary the play of light and shade on the *décor* in order to animate the scenes—effects, it must not be forgotten, that had to be achieved with oil lamps" (Gernsheim and Gernsheim 1956, 9). Striving for extreme "naturalism," Daguerre could convince an audience (through lighting and scenery) that a real stream or real tree or real grass was onstage.

Theatrically, Daguerre's masterpiece was the diorama, an exhibition of transparent paintings under changing lighting effects. Beginning in 1822 and continuing through 1839, Daguerre's dioramas captivated Parisian audiences. Contemporary newspaper accounts convey an unprecedented excitement and curiosity for Daguerre's realistic representations of nature onstage; for example, "The results are magic and justify the naive expression of a child who exclaimed that 'it was more beautiful than nature'!" (quoted in Gernsheim and Gernsheim 1956, 17). Others wrote that a new epoch in the history of art was beginning; yet another, in 1824, claimed that Daguerre's achievement was not mere representation but reality itself!

Although his biographers admit that the reasons for and particulars about Daguerre's initial interest in photography remain unknown, it seems clear that this interest would flow from his work as theatrical illusionist and professional artist. As an acclaimed wizard in optical manipulation and in the re-presentation of reality, Daguerre seemed destined to pursue such an obvious extension of his professional accomplishments, that is, the greatest illusion of all—the permanent reproduction of pictures of man, nature, and the world in general through the emanations of light.

In the 1820s Daguerre convinced Niépce that they should collaborate. Daguerre, however, realigned Niépce's priorities by maintaining that pictures from nature—not from engravings—should be the focus of his research. After Niépce's death Daguerre uncovered the possibility of forming a latent image on iodized silver to be developed or brought out after the exposure had been made. By 1837 Daguerre had begun the business of selling and promoting his discovery. The result was the 1839 agreement with the government of France to secure the secrets of Daguerre's work not only relating to the daguerreotype but also to the diorama. A bill to purchase the inventions was presented on 15 June 1839 by the minister of the interior, who cited a wide array of practical uses: "this most perfect reproduction of nature" would assist even the most skillful draughtsmen and painters; the art of engraving would derive fresh and important benefits; and the traveler, the archaeologist, and the naturalist would find it indispensable by "immediately obtain[ing] an exact *facsimile*" of his view or object of study (Goldberg 1981, 32).

Daguerréotypomania seized Europe, England, and America: news, information, and experimentation spread with unprecedented celerity. At first Daguerre gave demonstrations of the process, but in 1840 he retired with his wife to the country, where "he received important visitors from all over the world, and produced another triumph in artistic deception. He painted in the village church, behind the High Altar, a continuation of the nave in such perfect perspective that the unwary visitor is deceived into thinking the church almost twice its actual length" (Gernsheim 1982, 50).

The daguerreotype dominated photography from 1839 to approximately 1860. The process entailed a highly polished copper plate whose surface had been silvered and then made light sensitive with iodine or bromine vapor. After the plate had been exposed, it was developed in mercury vapor and then fixed with sodium thiosulfate. The result was an image of truly remarkable clarity and precise detail. To protect its extremely delicate surface, a daguerreotype plate was mounted behind glass. This direct positive process created unique images not easily capable of reproduction.

The jewellike quality of a daguerreotype was Daguerre's ultimate tour de force. A daguerreotype plate must be held at an angle to a sufficiently dark surface or the shadows reflect back at the viewer and the tones of the image appear reversed. When held correctly, however, the shadows recede, because they act as a mirror reflecting a "'virtual image': an image that appears to come from behind the plane of the reflecting surface" (Crawford 1979, 27). Daguerreotypes were treasured objects as well as mementos. They held the captured light of loved ones and favorite scenes in a device requiring careful manipulation and observation—a process, however, considered magical and thrilling. Daguerre had succeeded in giving the public the ultimate re-creation of nature—one that lasted more than just a short while in a darkened theater: it was, instead, a re-creation to be possessed and kept forever.

Although most late-nineteenth- and twentieth-century photographic historians and critics admire and sometimes prefer the quality and nature of a photographic image produced from a paper negative, as did some of Talbot's contemporaries, the Western world, at least from 1839 to the mid-1850s, preferred the sharpness of a daguerreotype. The polished metal plate of a daguerreotype accepted the layer of light-sensitive chemicals evenly; the irregular surface of paper did not. As a result, tonalities were often uneven and had less depth and richness than a daguerreotype, and details were simply not as striking. The paper negative produced "a reflection of nature as though through a pool of water ruffled by the wind" (Jammes and Janis 1983, 10).

Although the daguerreotype and the Talbotype were both likened to the engravings of such noted artists as Rembrandt in terms of chiaroscuro, the daguerreotype afforded a much greater sense of novelty as a visual experience. Daguerre himself encouraged the examination of a daguerreotype through a magnifying glass. In these first years of photography many were startled by minuteness of detail that before had gone unnoticed by the human eye. The calotype suffered by comparison, and although the process itself was new and astonishing, the results were reminiscent of engravings and lithographs.

> The first man who saw the first photograph (if we except Niepce, who made it) must have thought it was a painting: same framing, same perspective. Photography has been, and is still, tormented by the ghost of Painting . . . ; it has made Painting, through its copies and contestations, into the absolute, paternal Reference, as if it were born from the Canvas (this is true, technically, but only in part; for the painters' *camera obscura* is only one of the causes of Photography; the essential one, perhaps, was the chemical discovery). . . .
>   Yet it is not (it seems to me) by Painting that Photography touches art, but by Theater. . . . if Photography seems to me closer to the Theater, it is by way of a singular intermediary (and perhaps I am the only one who sees it): by way of Death. (CL 30–31)

Barthes's linkage of photography with Theater in *Camera Lucida* allies him to Daguerre and not to Talbot, for Barthes seeks an ontological understanding of the medium, so he seeks its creator. Daguerre created photography: it was the ultimate illusion. Talbot discovered photography: it was a logical development of scientific inquiry and experimentation. Once he discovered photography, Talbot worked to refine and expand it and to promote its practical uses. Once he created photography, Daguerre retired—not simply because he had received an annuity from the French government—but additionally because the illusion had been had and its initial impact could never be had again (not even with the development of the motion picture or color film, according to Barthes).

That one should categorize these individuals and their approaches so strictly is a convenience for the discussion of the various mythologies concerning photography in the Western world. Barthes cannot go back to 1839 and view photography as a naive man, except that he has to partake of one of the two dominant mythologies regarding the medium. Barthes is not struck by the marvel of this invention as a product of scientific accomplishment; rather, he senses the mystery of a chemical process that allows light to be captured in a tangible form.

Barthes's assertion that the ghost of painting has historically been photography's tormentor is quite accurate, although at first the opposite appeared to be true: photography seemed to usurp painting and drawing.

Many challenged the need for painting to attempt to reproduce reality on canvas when photography provided an apparently "seamless" visible transfer of the real world onto metal or paper. Truth in visual representation began to be redefined. Consider, for example, the appraisal of Edgar Allan Poe concerning this new medium.

> When taken out, the plate does not at first appear to have received a definite impression—some short processes, however, develope [*sic*] it in the most miraculous beauty. All language must fall short of conveying any just idea of the truth, and this will not appear so wonderful when we reflect that the source of vision itself has been, in this instance, the designer. Perhaps, if we imagine the distinctness with which an object is reflected in a positively perfect mirror, we come as near the reality as by any other means. For, in truth, the Daguerreotyped plate is infinitely (we use the term advisedly) is *infinitely* more accurate in its representation that any painting by human hands. If we examine a work of ordinary art, by means of a powerful microscope, all traces of resemblance to nature will disappear—but the closest scrutiny of the photogenic drawing discloses only a more absolute truth, a more perfect identity of aspect with the thing represented. The variations of shade, and the gradations of both linear and aerial perspective are those of truth itself in the supremeness of its perfection. (Trachtenberg 1980, 38)

One of the most famous statements circulating in 1839 about photography is attributed to the painter Paul Delaroche: "From today painting is dead!" Delaroche did, in fact, immediately comment on the relation between art and photography, although he does not convey the apparent antipathy suggested in the former statement.

> Mr. Daguerre's process completely satisfies art's every need, as the results prove. It carries some of its basic qualities to such perfection that it will become for even the most skillful painters a subject for observation and study. The drawings obtained by this means are at once remarkable for the perfection of details and for the richness and harmony of the whole. Nature is reproduced in them not only with truth, but with art. The correctness of line, precision of form, is as complete as possible, and yet, at the same time, broad energetic modeling is to be found in them as well as a total impression equally

rich in tone and in effect. The rules of aerial perspective are as scrupulously observed as those of linear perspective. Color is translated with so much truth that its absence is forgotten. The painter, therefore, will find this technique a rapid way of making collections of studies he could otherwise obtain only with much time and trouble and, whatever his talents might be, in a far less perfect manner. (Quoted in Rudisill 1971, 41)

But reaction to the enthusiasm for photography's "truth" quickly arose. As advocates for the traditional graphic arts began to argue in their favor, photography was denigrated specifically for its inability to approach art. For approximately the past 140 years many advocates and practitioners of photography have sought to overcome the view that photography is not an art. As important and as pervasive as these discussions were and continue to be, they represent a struggle that Barthes believes is not intrinsic to the uniqueness or novelty of photography. Nor is Barthes in search of the Platonic essence of the photograph, as the rhetoric of one of Susan Sontag's most famous essays on photography invokes. In "Plato's Cave" Sontag refers to "the essence behind the shadows on the wall," suggesting that photographs may be perceived as "copies of copies" in a Platonic sense. The idea of the "copy" is part of the photography/painting debate that Barthes skillfully maneuvers around yet ultimately moves beyond.

Barthes himself claims to approach his consideration of photography from a phenomenological point of view; he dedicates *Camera Lucida* to Jean-Paul Sartre's *L'imaginaire*. The *essence* that Barthes seeks refers to the phenomenological difference that uniquely defines or characterizes photography and differentiates it from other visual media. Barthes himself acknowledges that photographers will be disappointed with his book. His interest, at this time, does not lie with the choices that the operator makes when taking a photograph: these concerns relate to perspective, composition, tonalities, and various criteria that ultimately refer to aesthetics. Instead, Barthes employs the rhetoric of philosophy as he begins his investigation on photography. Like René Descartes, Barthes moves from a position of doubt at the beginning of *Camera Lucida*—"I wanted to learn at all costs what Photography was 'in itself,' by what essential feature it was to be distinguished from the community of images. Such a desire really meant that beyond the evidence provided by technology and usage, and despite its tremendous contemporary expansion, I wasn't sure that Photography existed, that it had a 'genius' of its own" (CL 3)—to a position of self-assurance that he knows the *ecstasy* of the photograph and knows that he has confronted or experienced the photograph's intractable reality.

Barthes's "note on photography" is clearly rooted in French cultural history. This grounding refers to a mythology that is formulated around the metaphor of mirror and illusion and the metaphor of mask and death. Coupled with a philosophical tradition that is crystallized by Descartes, Barthes can only see the ontological essence of photography through the lens of its mythological birth: his sensibilities emanate or, at least, coincide with the mythologies that took shape in the first two decades of photography's public existence. Among them was the sense that photography possessed a special ability to record not only historical persons and events but also family and friends. An article in the *Edinburgh Review* from January 1843 expounds:

> Even in the narrower, though not less hallowed, sphere of the affections, where the magic names of kindred and home are inscribed, what a deep interest do the realities of photography excite! In the transition forms of his offspring, which links infancy with manhood, the parent will discover the traces of his own mortality; and in the successive phases which mark the sunset of life, the child, in its turn, will read the lesson that his pilgrimage too has a period which must close. (Goldberg 1981, 65)

The latter point did not escape Elizabeth Barrett Browning in 1843. In a letter to a friend, she wrote:

> My dearest Miss Mitford, do you know anything about that wonderful invention of the day, called the Daguerrotype? —that is, have you seen any portraits produced by means of it? Think of a man sitting down in the sun and leaving his facsimile in all its full completion of outline and shadow, stedfast on a plate, at the end of a minute and a half! The Mesmeric disembodiment of spirits strikes one as a degree less marvellous. And several of these wonderful portraits . . . like engravings— only exquisite and delicate beyond the work of graver—have I seen lately—longing to have such a memorial of every Being dear to me in the world. It is not merely the likeness which is precious in such cases—but the association, and the sense of nearness involved in the thing . . . the fact of the *very shadow of the person* lying there fixed for

ever! It is the very sanctification of portraits I think—and it is not at all
monstrous in me to say what my brothers cry out against so vehe-
mently, . . . that I would rather have such a memorial of one I dearly
loved, than the noblest Artist's work ever produced. I do not say so in
respect (or disrespect) to *Art,* but for *Love's* sake. (Browning 1954,
208–9)

Browning eloquently testifies to the conflict that remains between art and
photography. The medium of photography is not simply a more accurate
form of portraiture or visual documentation: its very nature takes from the
living or actual object its own emanations of light. For Browning this
capturing holds more sentimentally than an artist's rendering of the loved
one. The seeming tangibility that a photograph provides of the thing
photographed bespeaks a permanence or reality not usually associated with a
painting or drawing. Although it is in *Camera Lucida* that Barthes's mythology of the photograph completely converges with Browning's, he takes a
portentous step in "The Photographic Message" regarding the difference
between photography and other visual media. He argues that all imitative
"arts" comprise two messages: "a *denoted* message, which is the *analogon*
itself, and a *connoted* message, which is the way in which the society
represents, to a certain extent, what it thinks of the *analogon*" (RF 6). The
point, however, is that "this duality of messages is obvious in all reproductions which are not photographic" (RF 6). The "exactitude" of any drawing
or painting is immediately turned into a style (Barthes uses the example of
"hyper-realism"). The photograph, on the other hand, transmits "denotation" to such a extent or plenitude that "the description of a photograph is
literally impossible; for to *describe* consists precisely in joining to the denoted
message a second message or relay, drawn from a code which is language and
which inevitably constitutes, whatever care is taken to be exact, a connotation in relation to the photographic analogue" (RF 7). So the drawing can
never escape the presence of the hand of the artist and her culture; the
photograph, however, apparently can.

After an initial period of excitement and novelty for the photograph,
photographers, coupled with their supporters and their detractors, waffled
as to the photograph's true nature and purpose. The daguerreotype was seen
by many as being *too* accurate, too unflattering. At first photography was
viewed as Nature's pencil and signified Nature's ability to reproduce herself;
negative reaction to this point of view, however, was not long in coming. In

1860 Philip Gilbert Hamerton wrote that "Nature's power of light is like a great organ with all its vast range of octaves. The photograph's power of light in comparison, something like a voice, but a voice of extremely limited compass" (Weaver 1989, 99). Hamerton represents one of many attitudes expressed in the mid-1800s in support of traditional graphic art over photography.

> Now what is painting? It is an intellectual and emotional interpreta-tion of Nature, by means of carefully balanced and cunningly subdi-vided hues. Its powers of *imitation* are extremely limited. However, the eye of the painter, instead of being insensible to everything that is yellow, is as sensitive to gold and orange as to blue, so that in this respect he may do truer work. And in this way of interpreting Nature's light, he has opportunities of compromise and compensation which the unthinking photograph cannot have. So he gets more truths. (Weaver 1989, 99)

In *Camera Lucida,* however, Barthes does not appear to concern himself with such possibilities; rather, he explores the myth that Browning so poignantly articulates in her letter. The sense of "truth" that Hamerton, for example, elevates—truth that he claims escapes the limited power of the camera—is sidestepped by Barthes yet ironically casts a shadow on the text by the very fact of its omission. How can a photographer—Nadar, for example, or the photographer of the Winter Garden portrait—be a mediator of a truth? Barthes makes this claim in *Camera Lucida;* he even explains the nature of the "truth" that he finds in certain photographs; but he fails to explicate how the photographer functions in relation to this "capturing" or conveyance of truth. Ultimately, this disregard seems bound to the fact that Barthes does not fundamentally define the medium (and, frankly, never has) in terms of the operator and the operator's style.

> It is often said that it was the painters who invented Photography (by bequeathing it their framing, the Albertian perspective, and the optic of the *camera obscura*). I say: no, it was the chemists. For the *noeme* "That-has-been" was possible only on the day when a scientific circumstance (the discovery that silver halogens were sensitive to light) made it possible to recover and print directly the luminous rays emitted by a variously lighted object. The photograph is literally an

emanation of the referent. From a real body, which was there, proceed radiations which ultimately touch me, who am here; the duration of the transmission is insignificant; the photograph of the missing being, as Sontag says, will touch me like the delayed rays of a star. (CL 80–81)

Barthes's sense of naïveté, of returning to the beginnings of photography, pervades *Camera Lucida*. In the section within part 1 concerning "he who is photographed," Barthes speaks like so many in the mid-nineteenth century who complained or simply felt uneasy about posing for the camera. In the early years of photography exposure time was long, thereby placing unreasonable demands on people who sat for their portraits. One of Henri Daumier's frequent subjects for caricature was the vise in which the photographer's client placed his or her head while the several minutes required for the exposure elapsed. Barthes recognizes that he cannot really complain about the length of time for photographic exposures in the twentieth century, yet even a moment of posing conveys a sense of lifelessness and/or inauthenticity that he, at least, feels as subject. The inauthenticity noted by Barthes when he sits for his portrait and which increases in proportion to the length of the exposure may be contrasted with Walter Benjamin's contention in "A Short History of Photography" that the long exposure time required in the early years of photography "caused the models to live, not *out of* the instant, but *into* it; during the long exposure they grew, as it were, into the image" (Benjamin 1977, 48). The path of immobility required for the photographic portrait smacks of death to Barthes but suggests immortality to Benjamin when exposure time is long ("Everything in these early pictures was set up to last. . . . It [a coat] enters almost unnoticed into immortality" [Benjamin 1977, 48]).

Barthes writes of an unspoken struggle between himself as subject and the photographer as "taker." Who is the creator of his photographic image—the photographer, he as subject, or what? Or is the photographer or the photograph a mortifier, not a creator? "In terms of image-repertoire, the Photograph (the one I *intend*) represents the very subtle moment when, to tell the truth, I am neither subject nor object but a subject who feels he is becoming an object: I then experience a micro-version of death (of parenthesis): I am truly becoming a specter" (CL 13–14). Although European society of the late eighteenth and early nineteenth centuries had sought to retain an individual's likeness through the silhouette, the painted miniature, and drawings obtained through various mechanical devices such as the physiognotrace, the camera lucida, and the long-standing camera obscura, the photographic image represented a new entity, according to Barthes.

History again bears out this point of view. In 1839 the *Leipziger Stadtanzeiger,* for example, declared the invention impossible, since "God created man in his own image, and no manmade machine may fix the image of God" (quoted in Daval 1982, 251). European culture, in general, did not prohibit drawn or painted portraits (as, for example, the proscription in traditional Muslim religion against the reproduction of the human form). Yet the idea that a human form could be created simply by a machine or without human intervention struck at least one writer in Leipzig not merely as an impossibility but as sacrilege. What remains for Barthes is that difficult, somewhat mystical quality of the photograph that flirts too closely with death: with immobility, with theft or seizing, and with embalming. He senses this presence of death as the spectrum, and he ultimately accepts it: "what I am seeking in the photograph taken of me (the 'intention' according to which I look at it) is Death: Death is the *eidos* of that Photograph" (CL 15).

Continuing the motif on the chemistry of the photograph, Barthes notes that a trick of vocabulary states that a photograph is *developed,* but he submits that "what the chemical action develops is undevelopable, an essence (of a wound), what cannot be transformed but only repeated under the instances of insistence (of the insistent gaze)" (CL 49). For Barthes, this brings the photograph (*certain* photographs) close to the haiku: "For the notation of a haiku, too, is undevelopable: everything is given, without provoking the desire for or even the possibility of a rhetorical expansion" (CL 49).

What Barthes is grappling with is the ability of the photograph to present to him as spectator a detail or gesture in a way that overwhelms and provokes him like a tiny shock or flash of illumination, as characterized by the term *satori.* Not only does he seek to approach his philosophic inquiry on photography with "naïveté" and "outside culture," he also discovers that what the medium of photography can uniquely arouse is the reaction of "a primitive, a child—or a maniac; I dismiss all knowledge, all culture, I refuse to inherit anything from another eye than my own" (CL 51).

It seems that in Latin "photograph" would be said "imago lucis opera expressa"; which is to say: image revealed, "extracted," "mounted," "expressed" (like the juice of a lemon) by the action of light. And if Photography belonged to a world with some residual sensitivity to myth, we should exult over the richness of the symbol: the loved body is immortalized by the mediation of a precious metal, silver (monument and luxury); to which we might add the notion that this metal, like all the metals of Alchemy, is alive. (CL 81)

Whether as intertexts or collaborators across time, Barthes shares or re-sponds to the novelty of the photograph in terms of a kind of mythology clearly present in the writings of people such as Balzac or Browning and as a kind of spirit and fascination with photography that engaged Daguerre or marked his creation. Even Jules Michelet, one of Barthes's recurring sub-jects, referred to the photographic studio (of Nadar) as "this house of magic" [cette maison de magie], before which one proceeds as though passing through "the Valley of Jehoshaphat" [la vallée de Josaphat]. (The quotations are from Michelet's entry in Nadar's guest/client album at the Department of Special Collections, Van Pelt Library, University of Pennsylvania [Ms. Coll. 21, page 33].)

The nexus of these relations is the confrontation of the individual with the medium. "What matters to me is not the photograph's 'life' (a purely ideological notion) but the certainty that the photographed body touches me with its own rays and not with a superadded light" (CL 81). Commenta-tors such as Susan Sontag in *On Photography* and John Berger in his companion essay, "Uses of Photography" (which is dedicated to Sontag), extract the contemporary functions of photography from its very begin-nings. For Sontag, "a capitalist society requires a culture based on images," making "the camera's twin capacities, to subjectivise reality and to objectify it, ideally serve these needs and strengthen them" (Berger 1980, 55). Berger, on the other hand, asks whether photography can serve a different function and resist the societies and culture of capitalism. He argues that the current distinction between the private and public uses of photography should be transcended. As "relics of the past, traces of what has happened," photo-graphs, Berger maintains, can "reacquire a living context" (Berger 1980, 57). Yet this living context is simply a different—and seemingly more noble—ideology: "the task of an alternative use of photography is to incorporate photography into social and political memory, instead of using it as a substitute which encourages the atrophy of any such memory" (Berger 1980, 58). Barthes well knows and certainly acknowledges in his writings on photography the uses that Sontag and Berger describe. The distinction that he draws, however, is that such analyses merely tame the phenomenon of the photograph by categorizing it as a political tool, a sociological fact, or even an artistic medium. He searches the ontology of the photograph and reintegrates into the rhetoric of the medium the sense of magic, of theater, and of chemistry (and alchemy) that the artist/conjurer Daguerre evokes. This mythology affords the potential for a singularity of response to the photograph that the ideological critiques of Sontag and Berger either ignore or subsume.

In 1957, in *Mythologies,* Barthes criticized Edward Steichen for removing history from the photographs comprising the latter's exhibition, "The Family of Man." Berger also cites this exhibition but argues that "Steichen's intuition was absolutely correct: the private use of photographs can be exemplary for their public use" (Berger 1980, 57). He objects, however, to Steichen's shortcut of "treating the existing class-divided world as if it were a family" (Berger 1980, 57). The exhibition as a whole, therefore, was made sentimental and complacent, although this was not necessarily true of each picture. The phrases recall Barthes's essay in *Mythologies,* but Berger's piece concludes on the idealistic note that photographs can achieve a human memory that "would encompass any image of the past, however tragic, however guilty, with its own continuity," and, thereby, "the Family of Man would exist" (Berger 1980, 57). In *Camera Lucida* Barthes works in a different register—one that emphasizes the individual. He says that if one views a photograph as a piece of history, one remains separated from it. History exists as that which is constituted only if we consider it, only if we look at it: in order to look at it, we must be excluded from it (CL 65). Barthes now sees that photography's potential is to engage the spectator, *a living soul,* in an image that coequally exists *as* a living soul or entity. Photography can offer more than "History as Separation"; it can achieve "utopically, *the impossible science of the unique being*" (CL 71).

3. Correspondences: Baudelaire and Barthes

I always prefer to work in the studio. It isolates people from their environment. They become in a sense . . . symbolic of themselves. I often feel that people come to me to be photographed as they would go to a doctor or a fortune teller—to find out how they are. So they're dependent on me. I have to engage them. Otherwise there's nothing to photograph. The concentration has to come from me and involve them. Sometimes the force of it grows so strong that sounds in the studio go unheard. Time stops. We share a brief, intense intimacy. But it's unearned. It has no past . . . no future. And when the sitting is over—when the picture is done—there's nothing left except the photograph . . . the photograph and a kind of embarrassment. They leave . . . and I don't know them. I've hardly heard what they've said. If I meet them a week later in a room somewhere, I expect they won't recognize me. Because I don't feel I was really there. At least the part of me that was . . . is now in the photograph. And the photographs have a reality for me that the people don't. It's through the photographs that I know them. Maybe it's in the nature of being a photographer. I'm never really implicated. I don't have to have any real knowledge. It's all a question of recognitions.

Richard Avedon

Among the curiosities of *Camera Lucida* are its bibliographic lacunae. Walter Benjamin's essays, for example, are conspicuous by their absence in the "Références" that are printed on pages 185 through 187 of *La chambre claire*. Although many other noteworthy texts on the history and criticism of photography fail to be listed, the exclusion of Charles Baudelaire's watershed assessment of the "industry" in 1859 merits attention. Baudelaire is, in fact, cited in *Camera Lucida,* and like Proust and Michelet he remains a recurring reference (or intertext) for Barthes. Baudelaire is also a touchstone for such key critical thinkers as Benjamin.

In general, historians and critics of photography frequently cite Baudelaire but almost exclusively in terms of the section on photography from his writings on the Salon of 1859. Usually, little to no context for these remarks on photography is given, except with regard to the industrialization of France and the rise of the bourgeoisie. Benjamin, in particular, champions this analysis of Baudelaire's insight into the medium in essays such as "The Work of Art in the Age of Mechanical Reproduction" and "On Some Motifs in Baudelaire." In the latter, for example, Benjamin discusses the crisis of artistic reproduction to which Baudelaire, Valéry, and Proust bear witness. "The perpetual readiness of volitional, discursive memory, encouraged by the technique of mechanical reproduction, reduces the scope for the play of the imagination" (Benjamin 1969, 186). As such, because of "the stupidity of the broad masses" (to cite a phrase from Baudelaire's Salon of 1859 review) Daguerre and his "mechanical" invention are welcomed—at the expense of art and the imagination. Benjamin considers Baudelaire's concern that daguerreotypy diminishes the "aura" of art to be a signifying motif, particularly in the later poetry. This concern manifests itself in Baudelaire's growing melancholia of expression attending such terms as *look* and *eyes*. Benjamin asserts that "the expectation roused by the look of the human eye is not fulfilled" in Baudelaire's late lyric poems (Benjamin 1969, 189). This failure is a symptom of the unreflective belief in progress of the second empire; Baudelaire indicates "the price for which the sensation of the modern age may be had: the disintegration of the aura in the experience of shock" (Benjamin 1969, 194).

Benjamin's line of inquiry in relation to the writings of Baudelaire draws provocative conclusions concerning the relationship between the discovery, development, and public acceptance of forms of mechanical reproduction and the decline in quality of our cultural world. Barthes's path in *Mythologies,* as well as many of his essays in the 1960s, echoes such sentiments: his analysis or methodology, in fact, derives from them. But what has become commonplace in the critical community is to accept—without additional analysis—Baudelaire's invective against photography based solely on the 1859 exhibition and the direction taken by Benjamin. This singularity of perspective overlooks a complexity in Baudelaire's art criticism that resonates in Barthes's writings on photography and the gesture.

Baudelaire began his career as art critic with his review of the Salon of 1845. Although one biographer suggests that Baudelaire had no fondness for his criticism on the 1845 show (Starkie [1957], 148), others maintain that "there is a logical progression to be discerned behind the chronological sequence of the [art] essays, and this evolution tells the story of Baudelaire's response to the constraints of aesthetic judgment" (Raser 1989, 15). It is clear, however, that "if aesthetic judgment resulted from the application of a system, all criticism would be entirely predictable, and consequently, uninteresting"; rather "art criticism remains mysterious" (Raser 1989, 14–15). Although the review of the Salon of 1845 may not represent the maturity of Baudelaire's ultimate philosophy of art, it nonetheless reveals several of the concerns and aesthetic interests central to him throughout his life—most of which contain an element of the contradictory or paradoxical.

Many key words, phrases, and concepts that reoccur in Baudelaire's art criticism appear first in the Salon of 1845 review. They include *originality, reality* or the *real,* the *new, naïveté,* and the *heroism of modern life.* In Baudelaire's lifelong praise for the work of Delacroix, he addresses the importance of the artist's originality and finds Delacroix to be great specifically because of his search for the new. Baudelaire even goes so far as to suggest—in a positive vein—that Delacroix's use of

> colour is incomparably scientific; it does not contain a single fault. And yet what is it but a series of triumphs of skill—triumphs which are invisible to the inattentive eye, for the harmony is muffled and deep? And far from losing its cruel originality in this new and completer science, the colour remains sanguinary and terrible. (Baudelaire 1981, 4)

The expression "science" of art and the related concept of the "logic" of artistic composition are sprinkled throughout the review of the Salon of 1845. Yet Baudelaire is quick to balance any appearance of artistic formulas with the seemingly nonformulaic impression that a "great" canvas makes on its audience. A great oil painting, for example, will possess a sense of harmonious composition that appears to have been created in an instant: "modelling with colour, however, means first discovering a logic of light and shade, and then truth and harmony of tone, all in one sudden, spontaneous and complex working" (Baudelaire 1981, 4–5).

In drawing Baudelaire claims to find equivalent merit among Delacroix, Daumier, and Ingres ("We only know of two men in Paris who draw as well as M. Delacroix"), although he recognizes three differing styles and executions.

> These three kinds of drawing have this in common, that they perfectly and completely render the aspect of nature that they mean to render, and that they say just what they mean to say. Daumier draws better, perhaps, than Delacroix, if you would prefer healthy, robust qualities to the weird and amazing powers of a great genius sick with genius;

M. Ingres, who is so much in love with detail, draws better, perhaps, than either of them, if you prefer laborious niceties to a total harmony, and the nature of the fragment to the nature of the composition, but . . . let us love them all three. (Baudelaire 1981, 5n.)

Here emerge the seeds of a dilemma for Baudelaire, and they rest with the artistry of Ingres. To Baudelaire Ingres betokens the fragment and a faithfulness to the representation of what the eye sees versus the interplay of the artist's imagination with the subject of the painting or drawing. In 1845 Ingres's skill in rendering his subject matter overpowers Baudelaire's incipient misgivings. As a matter of fact, Baudelaire bemoans the portrait of Louis-Philippe by Henri Scheffer for its failure to reproduce the king's wrinkles "printed" by "toil and fatigue" (Baudelaire 1981, 20). "It pains us that France should not possess a single real portrait of her king. One man alone is worthy of that task—it is M. Ingres" (Baudelaire 1981, 20). Although less than a year later Baudelaire was to write that "real portraits" were "ideal reconstructions of individuals" (Baudelaire 1981, 38), portraits must also reveal a sense of time or history—a particularity—that "idealistic" images simply fail to achieve.

Consistent within Baudelaire's art criticism is the search for the new that for the artist partakes of not only originality, but specifically a sense of naïveté, "without any dogmatism of school or pedantry of studio" (Baudelaire 1981, 27). Just as Barthes works to pull out from under preconceived notions and attempts to take on an innocence vis-à-vis a subject, Baudelaire states as early as his 1845 review that artists should spend less time being artists and approach their work with a profound naïveté (Baudelaire 1981, 27). Baudelaire concludes with an anthem for artists to seek

the heroism of *modern life* [that] surrounds and presses upon us. We are quite sufficiently choked by our true feelings for us to be able to recognize them. There is no lack of subjects, nor of colours, to make epics. The painter, the true painter for whom we are looking, will be he who can snatch its epic quality from the life of today and can make us see and understand, with brush or with pencil, how great and poetic we are in our cravats and our patent-leather boots. Next year let us hope that the true seekers may grant us the extraordinary delight of celebrating the advent of the *new!* (Baudelaire 1981, 32)

In announcing his view of criticism in the Salon of 1846 review, Baudelaire contends that "to be just, that is to say, to justify its existence, criticism should be partial, passionate and political, that is to say, written from an exclusive point of view, but a point of view that opens up the widest horizons" (Baudelaire 1981, 44). Echoes of this sentiment can be found in Barthes, at least in his writings of the 1970s as well as in *Camera Lucida.* For Baudelaire the criticism that he approves "will be that picture reflected by an intelligent and sensitive mind. Thus the best account of a picture may well be a sonnet or an elegy" (Baudelaire 1981, 44). This notion can be linked with Barthes's characterization in "The Reality Effect" of "the great mythic opposition of the *true-to-life* (the lifelike) and the *intelligible*" (see Raser 1989, 112). Although in his last years Barthes suggested that writing a novel might be the direction of some of his future enterprises, the move to a traditionally creative or fictional medium was not necessary to adopt the principles of the true-to-life and of naïveté and to create work "from an exclusive point of view . . . that opens up the widest horizons."

One of Baudelaire's abiding tenets for contemporary art is that "all forms of beauty, like all possible phenomena, contain an element of the eternal and an element of the transitory—of the absolute and of the particular" (Baudelaire 1981, 117). With this doctrine he seeks to root the artist's subject in his or her own time and experience. Yet one of the greatest faults that an artist may possess, according to Baudelaire, is to believe that beauty resides in the exact rendering of nature in all her detail. Citing Victor Hugo's contributions to the Salon of 1846, Baudelaire denounces the artist's lack of creativity and subsequent inability to excite the viewer's imagination and offers Delacroix as exemplar.

> One [Hugo] starts with detail, the other [Delacroix] with an intimate understanding of his subject from which it follows that one only captures the skin, while the other tears out the entrails. Too earth-bound, too attentive to the superficies of nature, M. Victor Hugo has become a painter in poetry; Delacroix, always respectful of his ideal, is often, without knowing it, a poet in painting. (Baudelaire 1981, 57)

Baudelaire expounds a theory of art derived in part from Delacroix's own theories, that is, that nature is a vast dictionary to be consulted yet ultimately transformed by the memory of the artist (Baudelaire 1981, 58–59). "Exact imitation spoils a memory" (Baudelaire 1981, 80).

> True memory, considered from a philosophical point of view, consists, I think, in nothing else but a very lively and easily-roused imagination, which is consequently given to reinforcing each of its sensations by

evoking scenes from the past, and endowing them, as if by magic, with the life and character which are proper to each of them. (Baudelaire 1981, 94)

Lest one assume, however, that the daguerreotype—so typically seen as the cold and impartial re-presentation of nature—carries only a negative connotation in Baudelaire's thinking in 1846, one should consider his praise for a painting by Lottier: "M. Lottier, instead of looking for the grey and misty effects of the warm climates, loves to bring out their harshness and their fiery dazzle. The truth of these sun-swamped panoramas is marvellously brutal. You would think that they had been done with a colour-daguerreotype" (Baudelaire 1981, 108).

Daguerreotypes and photographs in general were regularly utilized by painters in the mid-nineteenth century (Scharf 1968). Not only do many artists' writings reveal their use of the photograph, but also the juxtapositions of actual photographs with certain canvases unquestionably demonstrate the acceptance by many painters of the photograph as—at the very least—an aide-mémoire and sometimes even the "sketch" from which a work is simply enlarged and colored (Scharf 1968). Some, such as Delacroix, ultimately find the photograph too constraining, for its very "copying" of the "real" conveys a falseness by being so exact. The human eye does not "see" or "take in" the physical world in the same way as the lens of a camera: the eye "corrects" (Scharf 1968, 94).

The portrait is a particularly important genre to Baudelaire—one on which he has definite opinions. To Baudelaire a portrait is "*a model complicated by an artist*" (Baudelaire 1981, 81). He states that there are two ways of understanding portraiture—either as history or as fiction (Baudelaire 1981, 88). The best of the "historical" portraitists provide minuteness of detail without either including or overemphasizing the insignificant or accidental blemish. The "fictional" portraitist—the special province of the colorist—"is to transform the portrait into a picture—a poem with all its accessories, a poem full of space and reverie" (Baudelaire 1981, 88). For Baudelaire fiction may be truer than history: a "fictional" portraitist may realize a model better than a "historical" portraitist.

By 1855 and his review of the Exposition universelle, Baudelaire has solidified his views concerning the visual arts. In the first place, criticism itself must be free of a system and should begin with naïveté.

Like all my friends I have tried more than once to lock myself up within a system in order to preach there at my ease. But a system is a kind of damnation which forces one to a perpetual recantation; it is always necessary to be inventing a new one, and the drudgery involved is a cruel punishment. Now my system was always beautiful, spacious, vast, convenient, neat and, above all, water-tight; at least so it seemed to me. But always some spontaneous, unexpected product of universal vitality would come to give the lie to my childish and superannuated wisdom—that lamentable child of Utopia! It was no good shifting or stretching my criterion—it always lagged behind universal man, and never stopped chasing after multiform and multi-coloured Beauty as it moved in the infinite spirals of life. Condemned unremittingly to the humiliation of a new conversion, I took a great decision. To escape from the horror of these philosophical apostasies, I haughtily resigned myself to modesty; I became content to *feel;* I returned to seek refuge in impeccable *naïveté.* (Baudelaire 1981, 123)

Baudelaire is returning to his own prescription, which he gave to the artist in his review of the Salon of 1845, and applying it to himself as critic. The aesthetic pundit ["le professeur-juré"], as Baudelaire refers to art critics who apply preconceived systems to their reviews of art, is a kind of "mandarin-tyrant [who] always puts me in the mind of a godless man who substitutes himself for God" (Baudelaire 1981, 124).

Ingres is pilloried by Baudelaire in this review of the Exposition universelle. An entire room had been devoted to the artist's works, and Baudelaire's reaction upon entering this sanctuary consecrated to Ingres is one of boredom commingled with fear. Lost is the childlike reverence at work when he confronted the paintings of David or Girodet. A negative sensation now takes hold, for "imagination" has vanished from the works of Ingres (Baudelaire 1981, 131). "No more imagination: therefore no more move-ment" (Baudelaire 1981, 131). Baudelaire has taken up a battle cry that must pit him against Ingres in terms of aesthetics, for he understands Ingres's work to be a product of a conscious aesthetic of the "real" devoid of sentiment or the supernatural. This lack of sentiment and the supernatural has already been linked by Baudelaire to the insufferable fashion for "progress," "this gloomy beacon, invention of present-day philosophizing, licensed without guarantee of Nature or of God—this modern lantern throws a stream of darkness upon all the objects of knowledge; liberty melts away, discipline vanishes" (Baudelaire 1981, 125–26).

In his review of the Exposition universelle Baudelaire first uses the word *correspondences* in the sense that is meant in the poem of the same name. It is also in the Exposition universelle review that Baudelaire unequivocally separates his aesthetics from the "realist" school of painting and "realist" art in general. Baudelaire's concept of the correspondence between the spiritual and the natural and of the underlying unity of all art kept him at odds philosophically with the perception or representation of nature as an end unto itself. The bringing forth of correspondences did not occur through the copying of nature but rather through the symbolism that art employs as mediator in the recognition of those correspondences. A work that merely describes is not art, according to Baudelaire, because a work of art must transport ideas from the natural world to the supernatural and/or spiritual realm.

Baudelaire's derision of daguerreotypy as expressed in the Salon of 1859 review is what is generally understood to be his absolute and exclusive opinion on the medium. Sociological and cultural factors, as well as the development of Baudelaire's unique artistic vision, seem to support the finality of expression offered in the review. By 1859 Baudelaire has separated truth, at least as he believes the public to understand it, from beauty. He contends that nature is the only thing in which the public believes, and, therefore, the public believes that only the exact reproduction of nature is what art should be (Baudelaire 1981, 152). Former graphic artists dominated the photographic "industry" of mid-nineteenth-century France: Daguerre epitomized this world. Baudelaire's diatribe against photography in the Salon of 1859 review is a political tract that appears to attack Daguerre as messiah of this new industry but remains more completely a denunciation of the public. Although daguerreotypists are coconspirators with the public, it is the public's unquestioning belief in nature that offends Baudelaire. Like Barthes, Baudelaire rails against the failure of the public to doubt, to think, and to challenge the world in which it lives. Baudelaire links this failure with the ascendancy of the belief in progress that specifically partakes of science and mechanistic inventions and discoveries. "Are we to suppose that a people whose eyes are growing used to considering the results of a material science as though they were the products of the beautiful, will not in the course of time have singularly diminished its faculties of judging and of feeling what are among the most ethereal and immaterial aspects of creation?" (Baudelaire 1981, 155).

Baudelaire may not have even attended the Salon of 1859 (Gilman 1943, 116–17). In one letter to his friend Nadar, Baudelaire claims first that he is currently writing on the Salon show without having seen it and then retrenches somewhat in a second letter by stating that he had lied a little and had made one—and only one—visit. Baudelaire professes to rely on a "livret" describing the exhibition for his analysis. The image has taken second place behind writing for Baudelaire: what there is to know about this exhibition and its contents exists in the political, social, or aesthetic philosophizing that Baudelaire wishes to make. Baudelaire has lost the naïveté that he had once asserted he was bringing to his criticism: he has become polemic. The Salon of 1859 review is a work on the philosophy of art, and therein lies its greatness. Yet to assume that its description of photography is an objective and thoroughgoing analysis of photography at the time is to confuse the metaphorical use of the medium with other kinds of inquiry, such as Barthes's "ontological desire" to learn its "essential feature." Baudelaire's denunciation of photography is a convenience to introduce the more important concept of the imagination in relation to art. It does not provide a complete picture of his relation to photography. Photographers, most specifically Nadar, were among Baudelaire's close friends, and Baudelaire was quite willing to sit for his own photographic portrait, for example, with Etienne Carjat and Charles Neyt as well as with Nadar. He even contributed one of his poems, "Le reniement de Saint Pierre," to Nadar's album for guests/clients who visited his photographic studio. (This album is held by the Department of Special Collections, Van Pelt Library, University of Pennsylvania; the holograph poem appears on page 25.)

Baudelaire seeks photography's essence or purpose outside art. Although such a pursuit may seem to diminish the value of photography, Barthes shows that it does not. According to Barthes, Baudelaire would not be wrongheaded to understand that photography's essence is not one that contains the "dream," a notion so essential to Baudelaire's theory of art ("Each day art further diminishes its self-respect by bowing down before external reality; each day the painter becomes more and more given to painting not what he dreams but what he sees. Nevertheless *it is a happiness to dream,* and it used to be a glory to express what one dreamt" [Baudelaire 1981, 154–55]). Barthes recognizes that like the haiku, the photograph is not a medium to make us dream: "The Photograph . . . [approaches] the Haiku. . . . In both cases we might (we must) speak of an *intense immobility:* linked to a detail (to a detonator), an explosion makes a little star on the pane of the text or of the photograph: neither the Haiku nor the Photo-graph makes us 'dream'" (CL 49).

Some critics have embraced the "message without code" rhetoric of Barthes and Susan Sontag to explain Baudelaire's antipathy to photography in the Salon of 1859 review. It has been contended, for example, that "before a photograph, naiveté returns, and one regains trust in a 'natural' meaning: one forgets the difference between signifier and signified, and this allows one to seek in the photograph the satisfactions of the real world" (Raser 1989, 136). When Baudelaire, therefore, "detects this naiveté, he correctly labels it 'idolatry'" (Raser 1989, 136). Such an evaluation of photography's *noeme* seems to elucidate Baudelaire's contempt for a medium that allows the public to satisfy *desire* (expressed in terms of the Kantian notion of *interest*) and to overlook *aesthetic pleasure* (an expression of *disinterest*). "Because photography is interested, it is not beautiful, but in 1859, beauty is not sought by the buying public" (Raser 1989, 137), and, therefore, photography represents an evil in contemporary society to the *imaginative* artist Baudelaire. Such analysis is representative of how the medium of photography has been perceived through the eyes of Baudelaire in his Salon of 1859 review and through Benjamin's refrain of Baudelaire's critique. Barthes, however, does not completely follow this laid-out path: the assumption that photography is exclusively a medium of carnal desire is ultimately too simplistic for him.

Barthes addresses the issue of desire in *Camera Lucida* when he treats a photograph (circa 1854) by Charles Clifford of the Alhambra in Grenada. Simply put, the image contains an old house with a man sitting against a wall on an otherwise deserted street. For Barthes, however, the image captivates his imagination and sparks an overwhelming sense of adventure and desire: "this old photograph (1854) touches me: it is quite simply *there* that I should like to live. This desire affects me at a depth and according to roots which I do not know. . . . I want to live there, *en finesse*" (CL 38). Barthes avers that "this longing to inhabit . . . is neither oneiric (I do not dream of some extravagant site) nor empirical (I do not intend to buy a house according to the views of a real-estate agency)" (CL 40). Desire in photography is seen as an overture to an undefined longing within himself and not a response to consumerism or an impulse for power.

Barthes cannot abandon the photograph to the notion that it can only be viewed as a vessel for idolatry: the representation of "things" that one wants to buy or own in the material world. Rather than discuss this notion in the context of Baudelaire's 1859 Salon review (as do most photographic essayists, such as Walter Benjamin in "A Short History of Photography"), Barthes draws his thread of inquiry through the concepts conveyed not only in other pieces of Baudelaire's art criticism but also in his poetry. Barthes continues his articulation of the desire elicited by the Alhambra photograph: "it is fantasmatic, deriving from a kind of second sight which seems to bear me forward to a utopian time, or carry me back to somewhere in myself: a double movement which Baudelaire celebrated in *Invitation au voyage* and *La Vie antérieure*. Looking at these landscapes of predilection, it is as if *I were certain* of having been there or of going there" (CL 40).

Although binary opposition excites and fascinates Barthes, his commentary in *Camera Lucida* suggests a redefinition of the Kantian duality of desire and aesthetic pleasure. This redefinition is facilitated by removing the issue of photography from the discussion of the philosophy of art. Yet for Barthes the elimination of the aesthetic question does not make room for the validity of explaining desire in Marxist terms, such as those at service in Benjamin's essay "The Work of Art in the Age of Mechanical Reproduction." His contention that "that which withers in the age of mechanical reproduction is the aura of the work of art" overlooks the distinctive property that Barthes uncovers in photography. In an earlier essay, "A Short History of Photography," Benjamin does discuss what seems singular or special to the photograph, and his argument partakes of the sensibility that there is something magical about the photograph in its validation of the here and now. Benjamin, however, uses this observation in support of the authenticity and power of the daguerreotype, specifically, as well as other photographs from the first few decades of photography's history. In so doing, he ultimately concludes that the uniqueness of the daguerreotype (and the length of exposure time during the early years) created an aura that does not really exist in photography any longer.

> What is aura? A strange web of time and space: the unique appearance of a distance, however close at hand. . . . Day by day the need becomes greater to take possession of the object—from the closest proximity— in an image and the reproductions of an image. And the reproduction, as it appears in illustrated newspapers and weeklies, is perceptibly different from the original. Uniqueness and duration are as closely entwined in the latter as transience and reproducibility in the former. The removal of the object from its shell, the fragmentation of the aura, is the signature of a perception whose sensitivity for similarity has so grown that by means of reproduction it defeats even the unique. (Benjamin 1977, 49)

Unlike Benjamin, Barthes does not focus on how the repeatable production of the same image by means of the negative–positive photographic process vanquishes the uniqueness of a particular print. Instead, he fixes his gaze on the subject captured in the print and his or her unique existence.

In several of his own writings, including *Camera Lucida* (23), Barthes refers to his admiration of and interest in an expression by Baudelaire, the "rhetorical truth of gesture amid the great occasions of life" (Baudelaire 1981, 138). It is particularly in the exploration of this notion that Baudelaire betrays a philosophic relation to photography that belies his stated antipathy of 1859 and anticipates later discussions of the medium, such as Barthes's. Baudelaire has, in fact, been likened to "a roving camera, the unobserved observer, registering the new realities of a changing consciousness," although his "critique of the invention of photography is inherently paradoxical" (Diamond 1986, 2). The notion of gesture, its place in modern times, and related issues are best articulated in Baudelaire's *The Painter of Modern Life*.

Much has been made of the relative obscurity and unimportance of the artist Constantin Guys as criticism of Baudelaire's inability to grasp the future of art that was within his reach. Why complete an entire monograph on Guys when Edouard Manet was working in Paris at the same time and known to Baudelaire? (This question is asked and answered by Timothy Raser in *A Poetics of Art Criticism* [1989].) Baudelaire's interest in Guys had been germinating for nearly a decade before they actually met in the late 1850s. Although *The Painter of Modern Life* was first published in late 1863 as a series of articles in *Le Figaro*, it "seems to be nearly contemporary with the 'Salon de 1859'" (Gilman 1943, 140). Guys was a correspondent for the *Illustrated London News* during the Crimean War but ultimately settled in Paris. While the Salon of 1859 review remains focused on the explication of Baudelaire's sense of the imagination as the "queen of the faculties" (*reine des facultés*) in the arts, *The Painter of Modern Life* focuses on the subject matter and execution of art as Baudelaire would like to see it done.

Baudelaire emphasizes "*particular* beauty, the beauty of circumstance and the sketch of manners" (Baudelaire 1964, 1) as the key areas that the modern artist should address.

This is in fact an excellent opportunity to establish a rational and historical theory of beauty, in contrast to the academic theory of an unique and absolute beauty; to show that beauty is always and inevitably of a double composition, although the impression that it produces is single—for the fact that it is difficult to discern the variable elements of beauty within the unity of the impression invalidates in no way the necessity of variety in its composition. Beauty is made up of an eternal, invariable element, whose quantity it is excessively difficult to determine, and of a relative, circumstantial element, which will be, if you like, whether severally or all at once, the age, its fashions, its morals, its emotions. (Baudelaire 1964, 3)

According to Baudelaire the pleasure that comes from the representation of the present derives not simply from the beauty of the composition but also from "its essential quality of being present" (Baudelaire 1964, 1). Baudelaire sees the trace created by style and fashion not as an object for scorn or derision but rather as a ghostly attraction, a past that can recover the light and movement of life and become present. As Barthes considers a 1926 photograph of a black American family by James van der Zee, he "[is] sympathetically interested, as a docile cultural subject, in what the photograph has to say, for it *speaks* (it is a 'good' photograph)" (CL 43). Barthes is referring to the *studium* of the photograph, but its *punctum* is "the belt worn low by the sister (or daughter)—the 'solacing Mammy'—whose arms are crossed behind her back like a schoolgirl, and above all her *strapped pumps* (Mary Janes—why does this dated fashion touch me?)" (CL 43). For Barthes the detail—the photograph's *punctum*—transports a work of sociological interest to one that, in the words of Baudelaire, "express[es] at once the attitude and the gesture of living beings, whether solemn or grotesque, and their luminous *explosion* in space" (Baudelaire 1964, 18).

Baudelaire's rhetoric in *The Painter of Modern Life* exploits the rhetoric of photography, whether Baudelaire intended this or not. His concept of the flaneur is qualitatively similar to one of the common stereotypes of the photographer: "a mirror as vast as the crowd itself. . . . He is an 'I' with an insatiable appetite for the 'non-I,' at every instant rendering and explaining it in pictures more living than life itself, which is always unstable and fugitive" (Baudelaire 1964, 9–10). Today it is commonplace to understand or have heard of the photographer's sense of desperation to "get the picture" before the moment has passed, the light has changed, the players have moved. The same quandary faces Guys, according to Baudelaire: Guys is "afraid that the image might escape him. . . . [Then] the external world is reborn upon his paper, natural and more than natural, beautiful and more than beautiful, strange and endowed with an impulsive life like the soul of its creator" (Baudelaire 1964, 12). In a similar vein, Baudelaire iterates: "It is the fear of not going fast enough, of letting the phantom escape before the synthesis has been extracted and pinned down" (Baudelaire 1964, 17).

Continuing in the nomenclature common to the photograph, Baudelaire declares that Guys's drawings will have become "precious archives of civilized life" and concludes that Guys "has everywhere sought after the fugitive, fleeting beauty of present-day life, the distinguishing character of that quality which, with the reader's kind permission, we have called 'modernity'" (Baudelaire 1964, 40). His drawings are *tableaux vivants,* traced from life itself, minutely transcribed on the spot.

Ironically, the very qualities and sense of mission that Baudelaire admires in Guys's work become technically possible for the photographer in the 1850s. The so-called "instantaneous photograph" made its appearance in the mid-1850s, although throughout the decade portrait photographers still tended to rely on some sort of headrest for their clients. In addition, in the early 1850s the *carte-de-visite* portrait, which allowed photographers to create eight to ten small pictures in one exposure and thereby greatly reduce costs to customers, was invented, although its enormous popularity (particularly in France) did not occur until 1859. It was in May of that year that Napoleon III, while leading his troops out of Paris to support the Italians against the Austrians, stopped to have his portrait taken by André Adolphe Disdéri. "For Napoleon it was brilliant stroke of personal publicity to make available to the masses cheap lifelike portraits of himself" (Gernsheim and Gernsheim 1969, 294). This event was also the making of Disdéri's reputation: immediately his bookings rose; his clients had to wait for weeks to get appointments; and he was appointed court photographer. The number of commercial photographers and persons working in the profession in some capacity was dramatically on the rise in the second half of the 1850s. By 1861 people making their living from the production of photographs and photographic materials totaled thirty-three thousand in Paris alone (Gernsheim and Gernsheim 1969, 295).

Such was the social backdrop when Baudelaire in 1859 wrote on the Salon exhibition and on Constantin Guys. What Baudelaire attempts with Guys is to turn the attributes that photography's practitioners and the public in general vaunt to Guys's advantage by claiming them for Guys and building on them. It may be that the most persuasive attack that Baudelaire could mount against photography was the delineation and elevation of the artist who most resembled the photographer—not in terms of his or her fidelity to naturalistic detail (à la Ingres) but by the vision, subject matter, and speed of execution of the artist (that is, the notion of capturing the fugitive in the everyday world in an instant).

Another champion of Constantin Guys was Nadar, who was the first to mount an exhibition of Guys's drawings after the artist's death in 1892. It was held at the Galerie Petit on 17 April 1895 (Gosling 1976, 28). The missing link or that which does not ring true in Baudelaire's published criticism of photography is the shared vision that he in many ways had with Nadar, a most popular and highly successful photographer of the time. Under Baudelaire's nose Nadar was not only creating an enormous archive of photographic portraits of the famous, he was investigating the Parisian underground—its catacombs and sewers—and recording them through the first known use of artificial light in photography. By the 1860s Nadar was in the air (in a balloon) taking the first known aerial photographs.

Nadar was noted in his own time for his use of the plain backdrop in his photographic portraits. He did not exploit his photographic talent to produce banal journalistic pieces or publicity pictures, and he rarely accepted commissions for deathbed pictures, which had become popular. Like Baudelaire (who referred to Nadar in *Mon Coeur mis à nu* as "the most astonishing expression of vitality"), he sought a truthful expression of his subject and eschewed the artifice common among contemporary photographic portraitists. According to one biographer of Nadar, "the trapping of a man's personality had always been his obsession . . . in his photography, his drawings, and his writings" (Gosling 1976, 21). As Nadar himself stated:

> The theory of photography can be learnt in an hour and the elements of practising it in a day. . . . What cannot be learnt is the sense of light, an artistic feeling for the effects of varying luminosity and combinations of it, the application of this or that effect to the features which confront the artist in you.
>
> What can be learnt even less is the moral grasp of the subject—that instant understanding which puts you in touch with the model, helps you to sum him up, guides you to his habits, his ideas and his character and enables you to produce, not an indifferent reproduction, a matter of routine or accident such as any laboratory assistant could achieve, but a really convincing and sympathetic likeness, an intimate portrait. (Quoted in Gosling 1976, 37)

For Barthes, Nadar is simply the world's greatest photographer (CL [68]). Even when the subject is intimate or personal, Barthes finds Nadar achieving more than the usual in his photographs. In his portrait of his mother or wife (no one knows for certain, according to Barthes, although Nadar scholars identify the woman as his wife Ernestine), Nadar had been the mediator of a truth: "he had produced a supererogatory photograph which contained more than what the technical being of photography can reasonably offer" (CL 70). Barthes regrets that Nadar could not be his own mother's photographer yet is thankful that one image—the Winter Garden photograph—bears the "truth"—the truth, at least, for him. Barthes understands the genius of photography to reside not only with its chemical magic but also with the sensitivity and sophistication of its operators. This notion is not a return to the "photography as art" debate, rather an expansion or enhancement to the search for the uniqueness of the medium and its undeniable hold over the human spirit.

Barthes characterizes two of his favorite photographers—Nadar and Avedon—as "great mythologists." "To transform the individual based on a mythic universality, photography succeeds by means of the mask, which ends up inserting itself between the individual photographed ('le spectrum') and the regard of the 'spectator' of the photograph itself" (*Roland Barthes et la photo* 1990, 26; author's translation). Since the art of the mask is "a mythification" and by that "a lie," it is only the great portraitists who—by acknowledging this lie—begin to approach the truth of the subject. "The mask does not seek to alienate the first signification in order to superimpose an external mythological signification, that is to say, finally to make us view the general beneath the individual, but on the contrary, to make possible a vision of the individual person, to depart from a generality (for there is only a science of the general)" (*Roland Barthes et la photo* 1990, 26; author's translation). A photographic mythologist lays bare the essence of the subject through the presentation of the mask of that essence: "the mask is the meaning, insofar as it is absolutely pure (as it was in the ancient theater)" (CL, 34). So for Barthes, someone like Nadar can mediate the truth of the individual, because he allows that truth to emerge from the mythologies or codes that signify the realm of art.

And here again Baudelaire and Barthes converge. As he takes his mother's photograph in the Winter Garden as his Ariadne that will lead him out of the maze of paths that photography tenders, Barthes echoes (but with a positive voice) the begrudging impulse of Baudelaire to seek his truth and the fulfillment of a heart-felt desire in the photograph. In a letter dated "Saturday, 23 [December 1865]," Baudelaire requested that his mother provide him with her photographic portrait, although in a letter from 1861 he had expressed that "photography can produce only hideous results" (Baudelaire

1971, 187)—a comment prompted by activities relating to the illustrations for the *fine* edition of *Les Fleurs du mal*. In the 1865 letter, sent to his mother in Honfleur, Baudelaire communicates:

> Lastly, my dear mother, I am mortally bored and my only distraction is thinking of you. My thoughts are always directed towards you. I see you in your room, or in the drawing room, working, active, complaining and reproaching me from afar. And then I see all my childhood spent with you, and the rue Hautefeuille, and the rue Sainte-André-des-Arts; but then from time to time I wake from my reveries and think, with a kind of terror: "The important thing is to get into the habit of working, and to turn that disagreeable companion into my sole joy. For a time will come when I shall have no other." It tires you, I know, to write to me. You gave me to understand as much in your last letter. Write me a line from time to time to tell me you are well, but only, of course, if it is true, for above all, I want the truth.

> I would very much like to have a photograph of you. It is an idea *which now obsesses me*. There is an excellent photographer in Havre. But I fear it is not possible at the moment. *I must be there*. You know *nothing about them,* and all photographers, even the best, have ridiculous mannerisms. They think it is a good photograph if warts, wrinkles, and every defect and triviality of the face are made visible and exaggerated; and the HARDER the image is, the more they are pleased. Also, I want the face to measure at least one or two inches. It is only in Paris they succeed in doing what I want, that is, an exact portrait, but having the *softness* of a drawing. But in any case you will think of it, will you not? (Baudelaire 1971, 275–76)

Although his mind's eye "sees" his mother, although his memory holds her image and their time together, Baudelaire moves from such reverie to a request for a photograph—not a painting, not a drawing, not a sketch. Baudelaire recognizes the varying skills and styles of the operators and can separate that function from the medium itself: it is not the medium that frustrates Baudelaire; it is the execution of it. Yet the rampant mishandling of the medium is not enough to cause Baudelaire to deny himself its rewards.

Following Barthes's lead in *Camera Lucida,* one may trace the *noeme* of photography in even the most conspicuous of antagonists to the medium, that is, Baudelaire. This tracing lies not through the association of photography with memory, rather through the near madness that it generates in our perception of and relationship to time. In his writings on art and literature Baudelaire emphasizes that "imagination is the queen of truth" (Baudelaire 1981, 156) and that "a good picture . . . [is] a faithful equivalent of the dream which has begotten it" (Baudelaire 1964, 47). Such statements bespeak a philosophy of art in which the artist or creator holds the pivotal place in determining and defining the art artifact. In opposition to the work of art—the product of an artist—Baudelaire cites the work of those who may possess a "good knowledge of the dictionary" but not necessarily "a knowledge of the art of composition" (Baudelaire 1964, 49). Those "realists," he argues, who "want to represent things as they are, or rather as they would be, supposing . . . [the artists] did not exist," seek to depict "the universe without man" (Baudelaire 1964, 49). They copy from nature, which is only a dictionary, and, therefore, do not create works of art that hold merit for Baudelaire. The realists make no connection, he claims, between the mind of the artist and his or her audience. What Baudelaire endorses as art is the illumination of things with one's mind and the projection of their reflection upon other minds (Baudelaire 1964, 49). Photography, therefore, does not reflect the mind but merely the eye of man. As a medium it corresponds to the less significant category of functioning like a dictionary as opposed to art. It fails to "open up amazing vistas" but rather (Baudelaire sets up the work of Edgar Allan Poe as an example) should spellbind viewers, making them think and dream, snatching their souls from the quagmire of routine (Baudelaire 1964, 87).

In a fascinating reconfiguration of terminology and concept, Barthes draws from the imagery of illumination and magic, to *retrouve* those very qualities for the world of photography and to reinsert them into the critical dialogue on the medium. They are words that inform—in all directions—the writings of Baudelaire, be they his reviews of painting or sculpture, his assessments of fellow imaginative writers, his appreciation for certain composers, or his relationship to his own poetic work. Speaking of Balzac, Baudelaire in an 1855 work says:

> The story is told of Balzac (and who would not listen with respect to any anecdote, no matter how trivial, concerning that great genius?) that one day he found himself in front of a beautiful picture—a melancholy winter-scene, heavy with hoar-frost and thinly sprinkled with cottages and mean-looking peasants; and that after gazing at a

little house from which a thin wisp of smoke was rising, "How beautiful it is!," he cried. "But what are they doing in that cottage? What are their thoughts? what are their sorrows? has it been a good harvest? *No doubt they have bills to pay?*"

Laugh if you will at M. de Balzac. I do not know the name of the painter whose honour it was to set the great novelist's soul a-quiver with anxiety and conjecture; but I think that in his way, with his delectable *naïveté,* he has given us an excellent lesson in criticism. You will often find me appraising a picture exclusively for the sum of ideas or of dreams that it suggests to my mind.

Painting is an evocation, a magical operation (if only we could consult the hearts of children on the subject!), and when the evoked character, when the reanimated idea has stood forth and looked us in the face, we have no right—at least it would be the acme of imbecility!—to discuss the magician's formulae of evocation. (Baudelaire 1981, 125)

For Baudelaire the enemy of art and the public's response to it lies, of course, with his notion of progress—the love of invention and industrial advancement to the extent that such things overshadow or even replace morality and spirituality as the transcendent virtues of a culture. Photography—the mechanical invention for creating images—represents the fruits of this loathsome progress to Baudelaire. For Barthes, Baudelaire's sense of progress is dated and impossible to redirect in 1980. What Barthes can and does suggest, however, is that the photograph—perceived by Barthes, in a sense, like Baudelaire as outside the realm of formal art—can convey the sense of story or conjecture that Balzac felt when viewing the painting described in the anecdote.

In *Camera Lucida* the most striking example of this sensibility occurs in section 35, the one entitled "Amazement" and the one that embraces a 1931 photograph by André Kertész of a Parisian schoolboy named Ernest. For Barthes this image holds the beginnings of a novel. It evokes thoughts such as "It is possible that Ernest is still alive today? but where? how?" (CL 83). As it was for Balzac, the image is an introduction to and testament of the narrative or story that cannot be unfolded in such media—paintings or photographs that are single-scene and visually realistic. Barthes, however, does not unite the two media, that is, painting and photography, as sharing similar properties: "no realistic painting," he writes, "would give me, that *they* [Polish soldiers in a 1915 Kertész photograph] *were there*" (CL 82).

Instead, he alters the possibilities of how we perceive photography: he testifies that a photographic image can evoke a response similar to that which a painting evokes for Balzac. Barthes alters the uses of the words *magic* and *illumination* to reflect what is possible to experience and articulate within the medium of photography: he offers not the magic and illumination of Baudelaire's ideal artist but the magic and illumination of reflected light that travels through and survives beyond the traditional boundaries or coordinates of physical time. Instead of photography being an art—where for Baudelaire the artist's mind and soul would have to be reflected in and conveyed by the work of art—photography (for Barthes) becomes a potential forum to transform or animate the spectator into becoming the novelist, the artist, the witness. The potential exchange that is unique to photography, claims Barthes, lies in the direct confrontation between subject and spectator without the obligation to perceive or understand that exchange through the "mind" of the photographer. Photography allows Barthes to assume the role of novelist.

By 1980 Barthes can be seen as perceiving his relation to the physical or temporal world as one that can only be described or reported through discourses—be they visual or written—that all partake of the quality of a novel. He begins, for example, his autobiography with the statement: "It must all be considered as if spoken by a character in a novel" (RB [1]). The novel—or, more accurately stated in terms of Barthes, the "novelistic"—has become a starting point or base line from which Barthes's writings of the 1970s spring. His sense of the photograph, therefore, has been reoriented perceptually. With naïveté Barthes can reclaim a piercing relationship with the photograph, for that relationship now places him (phenomenologically speaking) in direct connection with the subject and content of the photographic image. As he proceeds in section 35, Barthes inserts himself in the prospective narratives of several photographs: for example, "When I see the beach at Biarritz in 1931 (Lartigue) or the Pont des Arts in 1932 (Kertész), I say to myself: 'Maybe I was there'; maybe that's me among the bathers or the pedestrians" (CL 84). Photography offers Barthes an "immediate presence to the world—a co-presence," and he is quick to note that he is speaking of a copresence not only of a political order but also of a metaphysical order (CL 84). Instead of the genius of the artist evoking and reanimating the character or person, the essential nature or phenomenon of the photograph—its "documentary" quality, its "evidential power"—has the potential to resurrect the subject in the mind of the viewer. Such a connection is, however, a double-edged phenomenon: in viewing the Winter Garden photograph of his mother, Barthes loses her twice over: "In front of the Winter Garden Photograph I am a bad dreamer who vainly holds out his arms toward the possession of the image; I am Golaud exclaiming 'Misery of my life!' because he will never know Mélisande's truth" (CL 100). In addition, if a photographic portrait lacks the "air" (the subject's expression or look) of a face, it becomes a sterile document: "the air is the luminous shadow which accompanies the body; and if the photograph fails to show this air, then the body moves without a shadow, and once this shadow is severed, as in the myth of the Woman without a Shadow, there remains no more than a sterile body" (CL 110).

The opposition that Baudelaire establishes between art and photography is reexamined in *Camera Lucida*. Barthes resubmits the photographic duality not as a "matter of oppositions (between two words) but of cleavages (within a single word)" (RB 129). As expressed in *Roland Barthes*, "between words, and even within words, passes . . . 'the knife of Value,'" for example, "*artifice* is desired if it is Baudelairean (specifically opposed to Nature), depreciated as *ersatz* (pretending to mimic that very Nature)" (RB 129). For Baudelaire in his public or formal writings on photography, the medium is not only in essence without artifice (in terms of the positive value of the word), its operators have pretensions and seek to elevate photography to the realm of art. For Barthes, photography comes full circle—its very lack of artifice (in its essence) was initially puzzling to him, perhaps even boring and without value, but when confronted with the Winter Garden photograph, the evidential or authenticating power of the photograph cuts him like a knife—creates a wound. This authenticating power of the photograph can be discerned in Baudelaire's 23 December 1865 letter to his mother, in which he expresses his desire for her photographic image. As Barthes's other favorite portrait photographer, Richard Avedon, notes, he as photographer does not enter the photograph in the manner that Baudelaire insists the artist must in his or her own work. "It is all a question of recognitions," Avedon states; "what I want," Baudelaire pleads, is "an exact portrait, but having the *softness* of a drawing"; "my grief," Barthes acknowledges, "wanted a just image, an image which would be both justice and accuracy—*justesse:* just an image, but a just image" (CL 70). The photograph is that word and that medium that cuts both ways between sterility and fullness; between banality and ecstasy; between death and resurrection; between the triumph and the defeat of time; between the tame and the mad; and, ultimately and essentially, between "the civilized code of perfect illusions" and "the wakening of intractable reality" (CL 119).

4. Contextualizing *Camera Lucida:* "The Third Form"

We shall not cease from exploration, and the end of all our exploring will
be to arrive where we started and know the place for the first time.

T. S. Eliot

Camera Lucida represents an attempt by Barthes to write in a new way, an
attempt to be both expressive and analytical at the same time, an attempt to
balance these two conflicting impulses within the same genre. In *Roland
Barthes by Roland Barthes* several passages speak directly to writing—specifically, to a utopian form of writing that Barthes strives to create. Early in the
text (in the "A's") Barthes begins with a self-effacing critique of his writings
but continues by trying to suggest or locate what is truly significant in them.
"On the one hand, what he says about the large objects of knowledge
(cinema, language, society) is never memorable: the treatise (the article *on*
something) is a kind of enormous falling off. Whatever pertinence there
happens to be comes only in the margins, the interpolations, the parentheses, *aslant:* it is the subject's voice *off,* as we say, off-camera, off-microphone,
offstage" (RB 73). Barthes's constant struggle is to try to "triumph over the
dreadful *reduction* which language (and psychoanalytic science) transmit to all
our affects" (RB 114). He submits that he has "a disease," the disease of
seeing language. In this perversity Barthes cannot escape his perpetual
analysis or self-consciousness in the face of language: "according to an initial
vision, the image-repertoire is simple: it is the discourse of others *insofar as I
see it* (I put it between quotation marks)" (RB 161). He then turns the scope
on himself: "I see my language *in so far as it is seen:* I see it *naked* (without
quotation marks)" (RB 161). But what he then conceives (desires) is a third
vision: "that of infinitely spread-out languages, of parentheses never to be
closed: a utopian vision in that it supposes a mobile, plural reader, who
nimbly inserts and removes the quotation marks: who begins to write *with*

me" (RB 161). These musings reflect the ideas already put forth in works such as *S/Z* regarding the readerly and writerly texts, and they also anticipate Barthes's articulation of a new genre in a 1978 essay and his eventual experimentation with it in *Camera Lucida*.

In a work presented at a 1978 conference at the Collège de France and entitled "Longtemps, je me suis couché de bonne heure," Barthes ruminates on *une tierce forme*. This third genre incorporates the way of the essay and the way of the novel: a certain indecision of genres "which will accommodate suffering . . . and transcend it" (RL 279). Barthes demonstrates this phenomenon through Proust and explains that:"If I have emphasized in Proust's work-as-life the theme of a new logic which permits one—in any case, permitted Proust—to abolish the contradiction between Novel and Essay, it is because this theme concerns me personally" (RL 283–84). In viewing Proust as he does, Barthes finds not a model to emulate but a witness to his own struggle. As witness, Proust can serve as a sign of Barthes's journey but not as a map for its undertaking.

While Proust does represent the pull of the novelistic in Barthes's late writings, Jules Michelet proves an equally compelling witness. Unlike the novelist Proust, Michelet and Barthes reside in the literary world of nonfiction. The essay—be it short or book-length—is their genre first and, in fact, last. Barthes's analysis of Michelet is particularly trenchant with regard to Barthes's own complexities in *Camera Lucida*. The forward or introductory remarks, for example, of the 1954 book *Michelet* contend that Barthes's endeavor in this publication is to "restore to this man his coherence . . . to recover the structure of an existence (if not of a life), a thematics, if you like, or better still: an organized network of obsessions" (MI 3). Barthes not only has crafted in *Michelet* an unusual text that alternates between his own commentary and passages by Michelet, he has also demanded that it is through the recognition of themes and, thereby, through a thematic presentation that the logic of Michelet's writing and his ideas is revealed. "*A reading of Michelet is total only if we distinguish the themes, and if we can set under each of them the memory of its substantial signification and of the other themes to which it is linked*" (MI 203). In this way, a "reading" of Barthes, but specifically a reading of *Camera Lucida,* must be driven by the thematics of all his writings on the image and their related concepts and driven, as well, by the structure of his discourse. In referring to the discourse in Michelet's late writings, Barthes notes that it is "continuously elliptical, . . . he skips the links, is unconcerned with the distance established between his sentences (this has been called his *vertical style*)" (RL 195).

Barthes's "third form" also skips links: in *Camera Lucida* these fractures seem to appear between his stated assignment and his execution of it, between sections within the text, and between the two parts that comprise the work. In an ironic forecasting of criticism that he himself would receive regarding *Camera Lucida,* Barthes writes of Michelet: "for many, Michelet is a bad historian *because he writes,* instead of simply 'reporting,' 'chronicling,' etc." (RL 198). For many, Barthes is a bad commentator on the medium of photography *because he writes,* instead of simply analyzing, dissecting, and so forth. When Barthes speaks of "writing," he is referring not to style but to "what we today call the *excess of the signifier.* This excess is to be read *in the margins of representation*" (RF 198). Barthes describes Michelet's late works as having an "*erratic* structure which privileges certain blocks of utterance, without the author's bothering about the visibility of the interstices, the gaps" (RL 196).

In his explication of Michelet are the insights into and prefigurings of Barthes's writing in *Camera Lucida:* they comprise "vertical," "thematics," "excess," "gaps," "obsession," and "margins." These concepts signify in *Camera Lucida* not because Barthes writes like Michelet but because Barthes ruminates and configures within a labyrinthine space akin to Michelet's: a thread or theme draws the writer forth, a process that sometimes precludes the traditional logic (or linearity) of the essay and may suggest the flexibility of the novel. Escaping linear time is crucial to Barthes's "third form," which streams forth when "the floodgates of Time are opened":

> once chrono-logy is shaken, intellectual or narrative fragments will form a series shielded from the ancestral law of Narrative or of Rationality, and this series will spontaneously produce the *third form,* neither Essay nor Novel. The structure of this work will be, strictly speaking, *rhapsodic,* i.e., (etymologically), *sewn;* moreover, this is a Proustian metaphor: the work is produced like a gown; the rhapsodic text implies an original art, like that of the couturiere: pieces, fragments are subject to certain correspondences, arrangements, reappearances: a dress is not a patchwork, any more than is *A la Recherche du temps perdu.*
>
> Emerging from sleep, the work (*the third form*) rests on a provocative principle: the *disorganization* of Time (of chrono-logy). (RL 281)

"The third form" informs *Camera Lucida.* The translator of *Camera Lucida* into English, however, misleads by his use of the word *reflections* in the subtitle. Beginning *Camera Lucida* with the translation of *reflections* for *note* biases the ensuing work and vitiates the concept of Barthes's "third form" by obscuring the ultimate control and clarity of his enterprise. The French word *note* is not typically taken as suggestive of a plural. Dictionaries of the French language indicate that *note* derives from the Latin *nota,* meaning "signe, marque, signe sténographique, note de musique, écrit, lettre, remarque, annotation" (according to the 1975 *Grande Larousse de la langue français*). In the second edition of *Webster's International Dictionary* (unabridged), the first definition afforded the word in the English language is: "a mark or token by which a thing may be known; a sign; indication; character; distinctive mark or feature; characteristic quality." To be sure, additional meanings of the word are at play in the title, especially those that reverberate to music. But Barthes's choice of the singular *note* with its suggestion of *éclaircissement* is not conveyed by the English word *reflections.* Not only does *note* suggest his own as well his mother's singularity, it also announces the resolution that Barthes achieved—at least for himself: he had entered his paradox, his mystery, his labyrinth and emerged composed. With typical modesty Barthes states in an interview from 1980 that he chose *note* in his subtitle because *Camera Lucida* is a short book, "with no encyclopedic pretensions" (GV 352). He suggests that his is "just barely a thesis, a proposition. But on the other hand," he continues, "I'm quite conscious of the *particularity* of my position, which is on the edge of this scientific field" (GV 352). His edge, however, is no small corner of the world: it introduces not only the individual but also desire, pity, and adventure into a rather sterile world of analysis.

The methodology for his undertaking (his "assignment" to write on photography) is intrinsically bound to "the third form": it serves both as structure or genre and as locus of meaning. At the end of section 2 Barthes finds himself at an impasse: "not daring to reduce the world's countless photographs, any more than to extend several of mine to Photography: in short, I found myself at an impasse and, so to speak, 'scientifically' alone and disarmed" (CL 7). He begins section 3 with a decision

that this disorder and this dilemma, revealed by my desire to write on Photography, corresponded to a discomfort I had always suffered from: the uneasiness of being a subject torn between two languages, one expressive, the other critical; and at the heart of this critical language, between several discourses, those of sociology, of semiology, and of psychoanalysis—but that, by ultimate dissatisfaction with all of them, I was bearing witness to the only sure thing that was in me (however naïve it might be): a desperate resistance to any reductive system. (CL 8)

"The third form"—that which brings the freedom of creative expression to the discussion of a philosophical problem—allows Barthes to embrace and to shatter paradox at the same time and to elude reductive conclusions while achieving a personal resolution. In his essay "Michelet, Today" from 1972 Barthes laments the antagonism toward authors (like Michelet) who blur "the discriminatory law of 'genres'" (RL 203). Their writings, he states, are often excluded by "serious people—conformists." Yet in the clouding of separate genres lies the genesis of a space or condition of writing that lets desire emerge and be acknowledged. Barthes is grateful to Michelet "for inviting us to transcend the mythic opposition between 'subjectivity' and 'objectivity' . . . in order to replace it with the opposition between . . . the product of investigation and production of the text" (RL 198). *Camera Lucida* represents an analogous methodology or discourse. For the first time Barthes is able to overcome the "uneasiness" that he has always known of being "a subject torn between two languages, one expressive, the other critical" (CL 8).

Camera Lucida develops or unfolds like a mystery novel told from an autobiographical point of view. At one and the same time it functions as a quasi-didactic treatise and as a work incorporating the elements of fiction, as well as autobiography. A sense of adventure is crucial to Barthes and must exist both in the stated subject of his writing as well as the text itself. He fears the ennui of repetition; he fears his future (his future writings) to be a series. "This feeling [of repetition] is a cruel one; for it confronts me with the foreclosure of anything New or even of any Adventure (that which 'advenes'—which befalls me)" (RL 285). If Barthes is doomed (like Sisyphus) only to repeat that which he has done or said before or if he is to know, in advance, the conclusion of every excursion in writing that he begins, then the possibility of discovering something new seems hopeless.

Barthes's quest is to construct a perpetual flow of sensations akin to a rhythm, albeit a highly complex one: "systems of moments" that succeed each other but also correspond to each other. Therein lies the adventure and the confrontation with truth, that is, moments of truth—an idea that implies a recognition of pathos and has nothing to do with realism.

> For in order even to sketch such a thing, we should have to disperse the "whole" of the novelistic universe, no longer to place a book's essence in its structure, but on the contrary acknowledge that the work moves, lives, germinates, through a kind of "collapse" which leaves only certain moments standing, moments which are strictly

speaking its summits, our vital, concerned reading following only a
"skyline": moments of truth are the *plus-value* points of the anecdote.
(RL 287)

And as if to throw down the ultimate gauntlet to himself and to his critics
(his readers), Barthes announces in the Collège de France lecture of 1978
that he expects to break with the uniformly intellectual nature of his
previous writings: "It is important for me to act *as if* I were to write this
utopian novel. And here I regain, to conclude, a method. I put myself in the
position of the subject who *makes* something, and no longer of the subject
who speaks *about* something: I am not studying a product, I assume a
production" (RL 289).

The production of *Camera Lucida* divides symmetrically into two parts
with twenty-four chapters/sections each. The individual sections, however,
serve less as fragments (in the sense of parts broken off from the whole or a
larger entity) than as mosaics—pieces whose existence appears to precede
the larger work in which they currently reside. Akin to this simile is the
notion of "mosaic vision," in which sight becomes a compound of many
simple, independent visual units—a checkerboard of frames that vary only
slightly from one another and that afford a multiplicity of simultaneous
perspectives on what is essentially the same scene or object.

In *Roland Barthes* this approach is described as "the circle of fragments."
"Liking to find, to write *beginnings,* he tends to multiply this pleasure: that is
why he writes fragments: so many fragments, so many beginnings, so many
pleasures (but he doesn't like the ends: the risk of the rhetorical clausule is
too great: the fear of not being able to resist the *last word*)" (RB 94). Such
fragmentary presentation, however, does not yield incoherence or deny
textual organization. "The fragment is like the musical idea of a song cycle
(*La Bonne Chanson, Dichterliebe*): each piece is self-sufficient, and yet it is
never anything but the interstice of its neighbors" (RB 94). The ideal of the
fragment is a high condensation that Barthes likens to music (as opposed to
thought, wisdom, or truth, that is, maxim): "'development' would be
countered by 'tone,' something articulated and sung, a diction: here it is
timbre which should reign" (RB 94).

Roland Barthes by Roland Barthes is autobiography written as novel;
Camera Lucida represents the didactic essay *cut* by autobiographical narrative.
The autobiography in *Camera Lucida* concerns the written history of both
the intellectual and emotional life of Barthes vis-à-vis the photograph. The
effect of this mode of discourse is that "the purely individual experience
attains to universality: not by suggesting what Man is like but by leaving

each reader the freedom to choose his place in relation to the discourse presented" (Todorov 1981, 453). Barthes wants to cease being a terrorist— one who "impose[s] his truth upon others" (Todorov 1981, 453).

The complexity of composition that marks *Camera Lucida* emanates from Barthes's notions of *écriture* versus *écrivance* or of *Texte* versus oeuvre. Barthes refers to *écriture* as an activity in progress, in which the author has invested the self in the production of the text. *Ecriture* differs from scientific or parascientific discourse (*écrivance*) in its openness and sense of ambiguity and apparent contradiction: it is a text that demands the active engagement of the reader with the writing of the text. Barthes expands this duality in his essay "From Work to Text," in which he designates "the work [as] . . . a fragment of substance. . . . The Text is a methodological field" (RL 57).

Among the propositions that Barthes puts forth about the text are:

> the work is held in the hand, the text is held in language: it exists only when caught up in a discourse (or rather it is Text for the very reason that it knows itself to be so); the Text is not the decomposition of the work, it is the work which is the Text's imaginary tail. Or again: *the Text is experienced only as an activity, in a production.* It follows that the Text cannot stop (for example, at a library shelf); its constitutive moment is *traversal* (notably, it can traverse the work, several works). (RL 57–58)

Barthes continues by referring to the subversive force of the text in relation to old classifications. How does one classify, for example, Georges Bataille?— an apt question for Barthes himself. "The Text attempts to locate itself very specifically *behind* the limit of the *doxa* . . . ; taking the word literally, we might say that the Text is always *paradoxical*" (RL 58).

Yet another of Barthes's propositions for the text is the notion that the text "practices the infinite postponement of the signified, the Text is dila- tory; its field is that of the signifier; the signifier must not be imagined as 'the first part of the meaning,' its material vestibule, but rather, on the contrary, as its *aftermath*" (RL 59). And perhaps most important to understanding the structure of *Camera Lucida* as *écriture* or *Texte* is Barthes's reference to the text as plural:

> This does not mean only that it has several meanings but that it fulfills the very plurality of meaning: an *irreducible* (and not just acceptable) plurality. The Text is not coexistence of meaning, but passage, traversal; hence, it depends not on an interpretation, however liberal, but on an

explosion, on dissemination. The plurality of the Text depends, as a matter of fact, not on the ambiguity of its contents, but on what we might call the stereographic plurality of the signifiers which weave it (etymologically, the text is a fabric). (RL 59–60)

The reader, therefore, is at loose ends and must make his or her way knowing that the text is "semelfactive," that which occurs only once, without repetition or continuation, that is, without closure. Not only is the text a form of play, but the reader plays twice over: "he *plays at* the Text (ludic meaning), he seeks a practice which reproduces it; but, so that this practice is not reduced to a passive, interior *mimesis* (the Text being precisely what resists this reduction), he *plays* the Text; [and] we must not forget that *play* is also a musical term" (RL 62–63). In the musical sense, Barthes suggests that the reader must "play" a text like an avant-garde musical score: "it solicits from the reader a practical collaboration" (RL 63).

In writing on *Camera Lucida,* one can never exhaust the complexity of its composition, but one can suggest the nature of this complexity by pointing to layers of textual structure. Barthes begins his work "In homage to *L'Imaginaire* by Jean-Paul Sartre" and thereby insinuates a method of phenomenology. According to Sartre, "the method is simple: we shall produce images, reflect on them, describe them; that is, attempt to determine and to classify their distinctive characteristics" (Sartre 1961, 4). At this level (within this image-repertoire), part 1 of *Camera Lucida* depicts Barthes stating the philosophical problem—"by what essential feature it was to be distinguished from the community of images" (CL 3); reviewing in shorthand existing classifications; finding them all wanting and finding himself "'scientifically' alone and disarmed" (CL 7); and then resolving "to start my inquiry with no more than a few photographs, the ones I was sure existed *for me*" (CL 8).

Among the ensuing "hats" that Barthes tries on in part 1 as he considers his chosen photographs are "Emotion as Departure," the classification of "Operator, Spectrum, and Spectator," "Photography as Adventure," "Studium and Punctum," and a series of actions: "To Inform," "To Paint," "To Surprise," "To Signify," and "To Waken Desire." There is every appearance in part 1 that these sections are fragments that sometimes logically move from one to another but sometimes jump randomly from one to another (or if not randomly then abruptly). Yet the end of all Barthes's exploring in part 1 is his recantation. He "had to grant" that his pleasure was an imperfect mediator: "I would have to make my recantation, my palinode" (CL 60). At the macrolevel, therefore, another structure is set in play: the notion that part 2 functions as a retraction of part 1.

The source of the term *palinode* may well be found in Kierkegaard's writings. "Kierkegaard . . . said that it is better to write a work and be able to 'retract' it afterwards than to write nothing and therefore have nothing to retract. It is [a] movement . . . [that] Kierkegaard mischievously termed palinode" (Bensmaïa 1987, 64). The idea of palinode conveys well the utility that Barthes finds in juxtaposing shifting planes of perspective. In *Camera Lucida* Barthes submits that only through the coexistence of opposing "odes" at the macrolevel (which are then coupled with the flash points within fragments at the microlevel) can he begin not only to locate meaning for himself but also to impart it to others. The palinode, therefore, serves as a deliberate methodology, a part of the production.

The locus of much that is meaningful or vital in *Camera Lucida* exists in the trace. The trace functions "both in the reader's present (as he or she follows the linear movement of the text) and in the reader's past (as he or she seeks to complete the reading by means of what has previously been read—in the text and, in some cases, outside)" (Rice and Schofer 1982, 32). Between the macrostructure and the microstructure of a text is "an entire realm of intermediate structures and patterns: traces, traces of traces, networks of traces, etc." (Rice and Schofer 1982, 32). In *Camera Lucida* the push-and-pull between unity/relation and fragmentation/contradiction is crucial to its creation and its understanding. The use of the word *palinode* can be viewed as a signal that Barthes wants the reader to *glisser* between the two parts (the two songs) of the book and follow the shifts and nuances therein, while simultaneously approaching part 2 as if Barthes had a clean slate on which to begin again his inquiry on photography. He asks that one follow two rhythms at once: part 2 turns down a new path in the maze, yet it should never be forgotten that this path remains part of that maze. Some critics offer the metaphor of the tapestry and painting to describe Barthes's theories and style: "Barthes's elliptical style of writing [which] precludes the linear development of his arguments and exemplifies the spatial organization of meaning similar to that performed by an artist's painting" (Champagne 1982, 42). "Reading [then] becomes an art of combining the plural components of the text into a single image" (Champagne 1982, 43): it is a weaving process in which parts of individual codes involving temporal data are incorporated.

Paradoxically, *Camera Lucida* may be viewed as one of Barthes's most complete books, because the threads that it draws together pertain not only to those presented in the text itself but also to the threads of Barthes's writings in general. When, for example, Barthes elaborates upon his notion of *studium* (a new term for him), it is, in fact, an echo of earlier writings on photography ("The Great Family of Man" or "Photos-chocs") that examined the photographer's myths in which he as viewer was asked to participate. In *Camera Lucida,* however, this reintroduction does not dismiss the notion in question: it serves, rather, as a mental check that returns Barthes to the plurality of the photograph's use or appeal. At the same time, such a check brings forth opposition: the photographer's myths aim at reconciling the photograph with society; by endowing it with functions, the photograph is dangerous; but this is an attribute of culture, according to Barthes, which does not relate to his delight or pain. The introduction of the concepts of *jouissance* and *douleur* then becomes a repetition of the interests articulated in Barthes's essays of the 1970s. What is new, however, in these iterations is that the juxtaposing or combining of these notions yields a new insight for Barthes: the photographer's striving to produce a "lifelike" portrait is, in fact, "our mythic denial of an apprehension of death" (CL 32). The mask of theater (for example, the Japanese No mask) returns to augment the image that Barthes is drawing: "Photography is a kind of primitive theater, a kind of *Tableau Vivant,* a figuration of the motionless and made-up face beneath which we see the dead" (CL 32).

This example of "traces of traces of traces" continues into part 2 of *Camera Lucida.* In its first section Barthes announces that he seeks an image of his mother that is "right," that performs well as a photograph or presents a living resurrection of her beloved face. "Lifelike" has become a wound for Barthes: one that relates not to the photographer's preconceived notion of what constitutes a good portrait but to the photographer's ability to function as mediator in a process that returns the subject's unique quality of living to the spectator. But the spectator has now become specifically "one who *loves.*" As such, the photographer succeeds if (s)he affords the "one who loves" recognition of the subject: a just image. In *L'imaginaire* Sartre cites a photograph of "mon ami Pierre" that did not allow him to "rediscover" (*retrouve*) Pierre: "the photograph lacks life; it presents perfectly the external traits of [Pierre's] face; it does not give his expression" (Sartre 1961, 22). Sartre concludes that if he sees Pierre by means of the photo, "*it is because I put him there*" (Sartre 1961, 25); recognition becomes a series of three actions, "three successive stages of apprehension: photo, photo of a man standing on a pedestal, photo of [Pierre]" (Sartre 1961, 25). So, too, does Barthes find that in "going through" his photographs all but one are what "phenomenology would call 'ordinary' objects, were merely analogical, provoking only her identity, not her truth" (CL 70–71). Yet unlike Sartre's experience, for Barthes one photograph (the Winter Garden photograph) elides the three stages of apprehension and exists as a primary apprehension of his mother. "Finally the Winter Garden Photograph, in which I do much more than recognize her (clumsy word): in which I discover her: a sudden awakening, outside of 'likeness,' a *satori* in which words fail, the rare, perhaps unique evidence of the 'So, yes, so much and no more'" (CL 109). The expression of a sudden awakening that lies outside of "likeness" echoes Baudelaire, who admires the attitude and gesture of living beings and their luminous explosion in space. It echoes, as well, the quality in Michelet's late works in which he disorders the proportion of facts: "Micheletist fact oscillates between excess of specificity and excess of evanescence" (RL 197). This oscillation or disproportioning is the writing of gesture into historical discourse and is the site of pathos in his texts.

Upon encountering the Winter Garden photograph (and proclaiming it to be the center of the Labyrinth formed by all the world's photographs), Barthes dwells extensively on his mother and her death. The book, however, does not then become an essay devoted exclusively to her memory. It returns to and reexamines other traces, such as time and pity, and resumes and ends with the discussion of photography's essence. This recapitulation of one pattern of traces within *Camera Lucida* may be repeated and deepened. The single example serves merely to suggest the methodology of expression and thinking that Barthes offers in his production.

One of the ironies of *Camera Lucida*—and perhaps one of the reasons for its elusiveness—is that through his digressions Barthes comes to apprehend the photograph as that which is "exempt of meaning" (in the sense that he attributes to the haiku, for example). In past writings, particularly when Barthes's stated topic was photography, the idea that the photograph was "without code" was puzzling to him and usually led to a discussion of the political or ideological issues being served by the use of a particular photograph. Barthes would assert that the visual transfer of the "natural" world through the photographer's peephole or lens seems to verify that the image received on film, paper, or metal is continuous and without code. *Doxa* would then quickly enter his analysis, as he proceeded to discuss the uses to which the photographic images were put. The examination or contemplation of a photograph of his mother escapes the demand that Barthes react to *Doxa* when viewing this image, not because a sociologist such as Pierre Bourdieu could not claim that family photos are codifiable rituals, but because Barthes's knowledge of his mother is singular. When writing of "style" in *Writing Degree Zero*, Barthes refers to its having a vertical dimension: "it plunges into the closed recollection of the person and achieves its opacity from a certain experience of matter; style is never anything but metaphor, that is, equivalence of the author's literary intention and carnal structure" (WDZ 11–12). The singularity of style is akin to the singularity of his response to and knowledge of his mother's photograph: the individual body or style of an author—"a kind of supra-literary operation"—"carries man to the threshold of power and magic. By reason of its biological origin, style resides outside art" (WDZ 12). Barthes refers to photography as magic, not as an art, in *Camera Lucida*. It is because of this sense of magic and of the singularity of his response to his mother's photograph that Barthes finds himself in a position to determine or pass judgment on a unique truth. The photograph achieves that unique truth if the recognition of the subject (his mother) is immediate, unqualifiable, and "exempt of meaning."

At one and the same time Barthes "finds" his mother and "finds" another simile/metaphor representative of his interest in that which is "exempt of meaning": "(despite its codes, I cannot *read* a photograph): the Photograph—my Photograph—is without culture" (CL 90). So the essay serves both as a consideration of the medium of photography as well as a significant passage in the refinement of the philosophical or intellectual interests with which he has been preoccupied in the 1970s. What many critics have noticed and treated in *Camera Lucida* is the sense of violence and desperation that Barthes invokes after coming upon the Winter Garden photograph: "The Photograph is violent: not because it shows violent things, but because on each occasion *it fills the sight by force,* and because in it nothing can be refused or transformed (that we can sometimes call it mild does not contradict its violence: many say that sugar is mild, but to me sugar is violent, and I call it so)" (CL 91). Barthes reiterates that unlike Rilke's line "Sweet as memory, the mimosas steep the bedroom," "the Photograph does not 'steep' the bedroom: no odor, no music, nothing but the *exorbitant thing*" (CL 91). The madness and sense of hallucination that ensue from the confrontation with "the exorbitant thing" are not negative qualities for Barthes; rather, they express an intensity or power that separates the potential inherent in photography from the world of codes, which now seems "tame" in comparison. Phenomenology had told Barthes that the image is "an object-as-nothing," but in the photograph he sees not only the absence of the object but "also, by one and the same movement, on equal terms, the fact that this object has indeed existed and that it has been there where I see it. Here is where the madness is" (CL 115). The photograph becomes "a bizarre *medium,* . . . a mad image, chafed by reality" (CL 115).

As Barthes allows himself to be led by the Winter Garden photograph, he traverses a series of points that include the perception of the *noeme* of photography as "'*That-has-been,*' or again: the Intractable" (CL 77); the notions of "Time Engorged" and "Time as Punctum"; and the concept of

"Life-in-Death" in the photograph. These points reach fever pitch and converge in section 47. "I then realized that there was a sort of link (or knot) between Photography, madness, and something whose name I did not know. I began by calling it: the pangs of love" (CL 116). Barthes's term for the convergence of his thoughts is "la Pitié." The Photograph has become (or has shown itself to have the potential to achieve) that which is akin to "the third form," whose "'moment of truth' has nothing to do with 'realism' . . . [but] implies a recognition of *pathos* in the simple, non-pejorative sense of the term" (RL 287). "The third form" can also be perceived as akin to that which Barthes describes in *S/Z*, where he speaks of "*le scriptible*" and the reader no longer being a consumer but a producer of the text.

> The writerly text is a perpetual present, upon which no *consequent* language (which would inevitably make it past) can be superimposed; the writerly text is *ourselves writing*, before the infinite play of the world (the world as function) is traversed, intersected, stopped, plasticized by some singular system (Ideology, Genus, Criticism) which reduces the plurality of entrances, the opening of networks, the infinity of languages. The writerly is the novelistic without the novel, poetry without the poem, the essay without the dissertation, writing without style, production without product, structuration without structure. (*S/Z*, 5)

"Pathos" is that quality of human experience or of its representation in art that awakens feelings of pity, sympathy, and tender sorrow. As in the lecture "Longtemps, je me suis couché de bonne heure," Barthes cites Friedrich Nietzsche in *Camera Lucida* as witness to the notion of "gone mad for Pity's sake," as "I [Barthes] passed beyond the unreality of the thing represented, I entered crazily into the spectacle, into the image, taking into my arms what is dead, what is going to die" (CL 117). Pathos was also an important theme in Barthes's discussion of the quality of Michelet's writing. Barthes claims that by conveying the pathos of his time Michelet was able to represent "the *real conditions* of historical discourse" (RL 198). Yet it is this very gift, Barthes argues, that we do not "tolerate." In considering Michelet, Barthes recognizes a discourse "obviously filled with those apparently vague and sublime words, those noble and stirring phrases . . . which we no longer see [as] anything but distant objects" (RL 203). It is precisely the pathos that Michelet brings to his subject matter that constitutes a barrier and signals his "fall from grace" with today's intelligentsia. Barthes echoes a similar sense of separation at the beginning as well as toward the end of *Camera Lucida:* no one seemed to share nor even understand his amazement at "looking at eyes that looked at the Emperor" (the photograph of Napoleon's youngest brother, Jerome) (CL 3); and the critics, he anticipates, will deride, "What! a whole book (even a short one) to discover something I know at first glance?" (CL 115). The latter response is reminiscent of a statement made by Barthes in his 1971 essay "Writers, Intellectuals, Teachers." He declares that a "writer" (a word which designates a practice, not a social value) is "any sender whose 'message' (thereby immediately destroying its nature as message) cannot be summarized" (RL 312). Like the photograph that does not transform its subject matter and whose description is "literally impossible" (RF 7), the writer's output cannot be reduced to a series of conclusions or points: "a condition which the writer shares with the madman, the compulsive talker, and the mathematician" (RL 312).

As Barthes argues that Michelet was sincere (although his sincerity is a source of his remoteness to most today, for "what is sincerest ages fastest" [RL 204]), so can it be argued that Barthes must be understood as sincere in *Camera Lucida,* a fact that might account for the difficulties that critics have had with this text. The sincerity of *Camera Lucida* lies in his struggle with "the third form" to embody desire and pathos and not simply describe or point to them. But that sense of sincerity also resides in Barthes's obsession with the photographic image in particular: an obsession that can be traced throughout thirty years of writings. This thematics imparts a superadded meaning or context to Barthes's "note on photography" and simultaneously confirms and confutes one's sense that the essay is universal but also singular, that is, a discourse on photography in general and a eulogy of sorts for his mother. In *Camera Lucida* the note that he sounds is that the photograph can offer "immediate Desire (desire without mediation)" (CL 119). Barthes uses the phrase "immediate Desire (. . . without mediation)" to emphasize (1) his sense that the photograph is not a representation of an object but part of (or a form of) the object itself; (2) his understanding of time when confronting a photograph not as memory (the time or object remembered) but as "*le réel passé*"; and (3) his search to abolish "les images" and to defy the common "impression of nauseated boredom, as if the universalized image were producing a world that is without difference (indifferent)" (CL 119). In *Camera Lucida* Barthes is not examining the object of desire but desire itself. Barthes discovers or witnesses this point through his consideration of the medium over the course of his writing about it. It is also by means of passing through his text that the reader gains the strength of Barthes's illumination: for illumination is not limited to intellectual enlightenment but also the white light of ecstasy, of rapture, that is, the state of being beside oneself, of being beyond reason. Ecstasy is personal and cannot be reduced to a universal formula or tenet. Barthes leaves the intellectual and emotional void connoted by camera obscura (a dark chamber) and enters a world of illumination (that is, the flash) marked by *chambre claire* (a chamber of light). "The third form" affords the integration of the intellectual with the ecstatic, with that which is beyond reason. It mirrors Barthes's insistence that the analytical world neither subsume nor ignore his singularity and *jouissance.*

The final section of *Camera Lucida* (section 48) is calm, even didactic, in tone. Barthes explains that "society is concerned to tame the Photograph, to temper the madness which keeps threatening to explode in the face of whoever looks at it. To do this," he continues, "it possesses two means" (CL 117). Barthes declares first that one may tame the photograph by making it into an art. He explicates his persistent sense that photography differs from cinema by acknowledging that the difference lies in the fact that "a film can be mad by artifice, can present the cultural signs of madness, it is never mad by nature (by iconic status); it is always the very opposite of an hallucination; it is simply an illusion; its vision is oneiric, not ecmnesic" (CL 117).

Photography can also be tamed, according to Barthes, by generalizing it, "gregarizing" it, banalizing it (CL 118). This sort of taming is what characterizes society today. Barthes, therefore, agrees to some extent with critics such as Benjamin that there is a tyranny at work with photography that allows it to crush all other images and that "we live according to a generalized image-repertoire" (CL 118). This generalization "completely de-realizes the human world of conflicts and desires, under cover of illustrating it" (CL 118). The consumption of images in the so-called advanced societies versus the consumption of beliefs in the past may make for a more liberal society but also a less authentic one.

Camera Lucida concludes on a very strong note: the two ways of the photograph pertain to either embracing or taming its madness, "to subject its spectacle to the civilized code of perfect illusions, or to confront in it the wakening of intractable reality" (CL 119). Barthes declares that the choice is his. He submits that regardless of the force and omnipresence of "l'imaginaire généralisé," he maintains the power of choice to experience "the photographic ecstasy" (*l'extase photographique*). Not only has Barthes come to realize the *noeme* of photography, he has also clarified that although the photographic *noeme* is submerged by society through generalization, it remains to be confronted, if the will of the individual so elects.

In contradistinction, Benjamin, although fascinated by the photograph, ultimately perceives the photograph as a medium that diminishes rather than enhances. In discussing memory in his essay "On Some Motifs in Baudelaire,"

Benjamin designates "aura" as "the associations which, at home in the *mémoire involontaire,* tend to cluster around the object of a perception" (Benjamin 1969, 186). According to Benjamin, *mémoire volontaire* is at the service of the intellect, and its characteristic is that "the information which it gives about the past retains no trace of it" (Benjamin 1969, 158), while *mémoire involontaire* is that in which the past is retrieved through an unknown or intellectually unknowable object or the sensation aroused by that object. Benjamin contends that "the techniques based on the use of the camera and of subsequent analogous mechanical devices extend the range of the *mémoire volontaire*" (Benjamin 1969, 186). He concludes that "if the distinctive feature of the images that rise from the *mémoire involontaire* is seen in their aura, then photography is decisively implicated in the phenomenon of the 'decline of the aura'" (Benjamin 1969, 187).

Although Benjamin's notion of the "decline of the aura" may be perceived in Barthes's views of *l'imaginaire généralisé,* the difference between the two writers with regard to photography arises in their respective views of the "gaze." Benjamin suggests that "the camera records our likeness without returning our gaze" (Benjamin 1969, 188). In contrast, Barthes remarks in the second line of *Camera Lucida* that upon a chance encounter with an 1852 photograph of Napoleon's younger brother he realized (with amazement) that "I am *looking* at *eyes* that *looked* at the Emperor" (CL 3; emphasis added). For Barthes the camera and the photographer serve as mediators, go-betweens that allow Barthes to return the gaze of Napoleon's brother. It is not important that the camera return the subject's gaze, because it is only a vessel to provide for the potential of that exchange. Although Barthes senses that he is alone in his amazement over returning the gaze of Napoleon's brother, he, nonetheless, acknowledges the existence of the returned gaze.

For Benjamin, however, the "gaze" and the "aura" are linked: "to perceive the aura of an object we look at means to invest it with the ability to look at us in return" (Benjamin 1969, 188). In turn, this experience corresponds to the data of the *mémoire involontaire*—unique data which "are lost to the memory that seeks to retain them" (Benjamin 1969, 188). Barthes would agree that his experiences with certain photographs do not pertain to *mémoire involontaire* as Benjamin describes it, because Barthes does not *remember* Napoleon's brother in seeing that individual's photograph. Nor does Barthes seek an "aura" from the photograph: he is *literally* not *remembering.* He does, however, return the subject's gaze in a circle of gazes that unites brother, Emperor, and Barthes, for, as Barthes exclaims, "I am the reference of every photograph" (CL 84). This return transcends chronological time and defines the photograph's *punctum* to Barthes.

Among the most noted and seemingly significant aspects of *Camera Lucida* with regard to the analysis of photography are Barthes's newly invented terms *studium* and *punctum*. In section 10 of the book he introduces these neologisms derived from Latin to denote the copresence of two discontinuous elements in the photograph. The existence of two heterogeneous components is most striking to Barthes in images taken by the photojournalist Koen Wessing in 1979 in Nicaragua. Wessing was reporting on this country's brutal civil war: his photographs seem to capture that brutality—that pathos—through their juxtaposition of the men of war (the soldiers) or their victims with ordinary citizens (nuns) or the friends and relatives of the victims. The composition created by heterogeneous categories does not, however, constitute the power or poignancy of the images: rather, it is the actuality of the individuals' reality as documented by the visual details that cannot help but be there in the photograph. In the Wessing photograph of the weeping mother such details include a sheet, a bare foot, and a handkerchief. These details exceed the conventional space or boundaries of visual composition; they pierce that space and defy the obvious meaning(s) that photographer and publisher will give the image or for which they will use the image. Akin to Barthes's dichotomy, therefore, between the obvious and the obtuse is the binary opposition of the *studium* and the *punctum*.

Studium represents the world of codes, of culture, of conventionalized context. It is not an unimportant world, and Barthes acknowledges in *Camera Lucida* that he appreciates and is nourished intellectually by culture. And undeniably, he is a product of culture—of education, formal training, and an academic or intellectual community that, regardless of how seemingly avant-garde, remains communicative and comprehensible because of shared language, shared erudition, shared antecedents, and so forth. In the realm of the *studium* Barthes's attention to (interest in) the Nicaraguan photographs derives from his ethical and political culture. He can expect, for the most part, a similarity of response within his cultural community. The concept of the *punctum,* on the other hand, speaks to that quality or state in the photograph that is not exclusively anchored in a cultural response (message) that has been engineered (structured) in the manner of a traditional "sign."

Barthes's introduction of the binary theme of *studium* and *punctum* creates some paradoxical predicaments. It has been suggested that the *punctum* can be viewed as that which leads one into the *studium* of the photograph (Craig Saper, Conference on Roland Barthes, University of Pennsylvania, 1994). Given the literally innumerable quantity of photographs in the world today, a photograph's *punctum* (that "accident which pricks" one in a photograph) can revive an image from the visual overload that makes us not "see" it anymore (in the sense of noticing or attending to its contents). The *punctum* can be that detail or quality which separates a photograph from the banality of our commercialized and propagandized visual universe. The *punctum*, therefore, is that point which draws one into a particular photograph and connects one to its historical context (its *studium*). Conversely, one could argue that it is the photograph's *studium* that allows the *punctum* (if the viewer is struck by one) to exist. If the *studium* is seen as those elements in the photograph that culture—specifically, history—contextualizes and ex-plains, then the *punctum* cannot really *emerge* from an image that functions as an intellectual or cultural unknown or void, because the essence of the *punctum* is that it punctures the photograph's cultural coding (its *studium*). If one does not understand or respond to the cultural context (the *studium* of the photograph), the lacerating detail and the photograph's potential for pathos remain obscured: without a frame or setting, there is nothing to be exceeded, nothing to be pierced.

Between the two parts of *Camera Lucida* the terms *studium* and *punctum* undergo a transfiguration. In part 1 the sense and utility of the expressions bespeak the analytical or didactic skills that have come to typify Barthes's work. Although introduced through a methodology that proclaimed its singularity, the words "sound" and can function in a somewhat impersonal, quasi-scientific manner reminiscent of the semiological and structural inves-tigations for which he is most widely known. Yet the clear distinctions put forth in part 1 between the dual terms mask the trend in Barthes's texts to seek or refer to a third entity that lies beyond the perimeters formed by certain categories or genres. For the photographs discussed and printed in part 2 of *Camera Lucida,* the field of the *studium* (as demonstrated in part 1) narrows, and the field of the *punctum* is pinpointed to the "very letter of Time" and its "defeat." The images include the Winter Garden photograph (not printed); a family portrait; a portrait by the "world's greatest photogra-pher," Nadar, with the provocative title "The Artist's Mother (or Wife)"; and a 1931 photograph of a young French schoolboy named Ernest. What signifies in this selection (which also encompasses the "first" photograph by Niépce and four portraits by acclaimed photographers of famous or infa-mous people) is Barthes's focus on the individual and his or her gaze. For the most part, these photographs overwhelm Barthes as certificates not only of the subjects' existence but also of their unique presence, their individual lives. By contrast, the images within part 1 are less personal for Barthes in terms of their subject matter, although they, too, prompt a certain individuality of response in him.

The "third form" allows Barthes to distinguish, explore, and embrace both the public and private worlds of photography and the public and private faces of his terms *studium* and *punctum*. Barthes leaves the reader with a paradox: he introduces nomenclature and investigates its functionality, but any systematic or critical appraisal of photography by means of these terms vitiates their essence. The *punctum,* for example, cannot be pinned down and dissected, because it shifts between one viewer and another; because it can even shift within one viewer's response over time; because it is not necessarily what the photographer has seen or "given" to the print; and because it is not a thing but rather a condition that arises from the *noeme* of the unique medium of photography: "That-has-been" (*Ça a été*). For Barthes this *noeme* holds both a cultural and a personal significance. The cultural import concerns our understanding of or relationship to history; within the personal sphere, the "That-has-been" of the Winter Garden photograph allows Barthes to do much more than "recognize" his mother—he "discovers" her. That quality of the photograph is, however, abrupt: the photograph (if "good," if "true") seizes a moment in time that conveys the reality of the individual (her "Look"), but the flash of discovery does not lead anywhere: "So, yes, so much and no more" (CL 109). Understanding or discussing Barthes's *punctum* only at the level of a photograph's piercing visual detail(s) (although the *punctum* most certainly is suspended by such details) draws one away from the overriding trait that marks the singularity of the form. Time as the *punctum* of all photographs is the unique interstice that Barthes contributes to the ruminations on the medium of photography.

5. Time: The Photographic *Punctum*

The photographic image is the object itself, the object freed from the conditions of time and space that govern it. No matter how fuzzy, distorted, or discolored, no matter how lacking in documentary value the image may be, it shares, by virtue of the very process of its becoming, the being of the model of which it is the representation; it *is* the model.

Hence the charm of family albums. Those grey or sepia shadows, phantomlike and almost undecipherable, are no longer traditional family portraits but rather the disturbing presence of lives halted at a set moment in their duration, freed from their destiny; not, however, by the prestige of art but by the power of an impassive mechanical process: for photography does not create eternity, as art does, it embalms time, rescuing it simply from its proper corruption.

André Bazin, "The Ontology of the Photographic Image"

If we wish to describe the *motion* of a material point, we give the values of its co-ordinates as functions of time. Now we must bear carefully in mind that a mathematical description of this kind has no physical meaning unless we are quite clear as to what we understand by "time."

Albert Einstein, "On the Electrodynamics of Moving Bodies"

The Barthesian proclamation is made: "This new *punctum,* which is no longer of form but of intensity, is Time, the lacerating emphasis of the *noeme* ('*that-has-been*'), its pure representation" (CL 96). It seems on the surface simple, straightforward (even banal, according to Barthes). There is nevertheless a dilemma, and it is Augustinian, that is to say, profoundly, incorrigibly definitional. In *The Confessions* Augustine agonized over the complexity of the proper understanding of time:

My soul is on fire to solve this very complicated enigma ["What then is time?"]. Do not shut the door on these things, my Lord God, good Father, in the name of Christ I beg you, do not shut the door in the face of my longings to know these things which are so familiar and at the same time so obscure. (Augustine 1963, 274)

The Augustinian dilemma is the perplexity of the beingness of time. How can one speak of a past time or a future time, both of which seem equally nonexistent? Does time come to meet one and pass one by in an infinite succession of "nows," or is time given all at once and one moves within it on a predetermined trajectory? Is man the rock in the stream or is he the stream moving around an infinite number of rocks? Following Einstein's lead, then, it must be determined just what is meant by *time* in *Camera Lucida,* for Barthes's age stands philosophically at a radically different place from the age of photography's creators and its first generation of practitioners and viewers.

Time has proven to be one of the great perplexities of Western thought. Barthes's linkage of the *punctum*—that sting or cut or accident that pricks and bruises—with time signals not only a potentially complex association but also an undoubtedly lacerating and maddening one as well. Indeed, time and our ideas of it intersect at every point concepts of being and of reality, of the continuity of existence, and of our free will to act as unique individuals. Time is the substantive underpinning, the causal link, in an otherwise fragmented and accidental world of absolute individuation. Time stands firm as the primary signature of consciousness. As A. S. Eddington writes:

> When I close my eyes and retreat into my inner mind, I feel myself *enduring,* I do not feel *extensive.* It is this feeling of time as affecting ourselves and not merely as existing in the relation of external events which is so peculiarly characteristic of it. . . . That is why time seems to us so much more mysterious than space. . . . We have intimate acquaintance with the nature of time and so it baffles our comprehension. (Eddington 1929, 50–51)

The quest to define and to understand the nature of time and its relation to being and reality has, as often as not, eluded the greatest of efforts. Although the philosophical complexity of time underscores *Camera Lucida,* Barthes's primary discussion of time remains with a physical time and not a metaphysical time: the time that engages the attention of twentieth-century science, the time of irrevocable physical events, and the time of human consciousness shaped by and imbedded in this particular worldview. Barthes himself suggests this connection:

> It is often said that it was the painters who invented Photography (by bequeathing it their framing, the Albertian perspective, and the optic of the *camera obscura*). I say: no, it was the chemists. For the *noeme*

"That-has-been" was possible only on the day when a scientific circumstance (the discovery that silver halogens were sensitive to light) made it possible to recover and print directly the luminous rays emitted by a variously lighted object. The photograph is literally an emanation of the referent. From a real body, which was there, proceed radiations which ultimately touch me, who am here; the duration of the transmission is insignificant; the photograph of the missing being, as Sontag says, will touch me like the delayed rays of a star. (CL 80–81)

Throughout most of the nineteenth century there was an ever-widening stream of dissent from the Newtonian picture of the universe—the world of a determinable and dynamic mechanism. Central to the problems leading to this dissent were Newton's ideas of absolute time and space and his ideas (for which the former were formulated) of a force acting simultaneously upon an object at a distance. Light was such a force, and, accordingly, light was, in Newton's grand design, propagated at an infinite speed. In order to effect this idea of an absolute time, Newton drew a clear distinction between the time of the senses (subject to error and distortion) and what he proposed to be the true and mathematical time of eternity:

Only I observe, that the common people conceive those quantities under no other notions but from the relation they bear to sensible objects. . . . Absolute, true, and mathematical time, of itself, and from its own nature, flows equally without relation to anything external, and by another name is called duration: relative, apparent, and common time, is some sensible and external (whether accurate or unequable) measure of duration by the means of motion, which is commonly used instead of true time; such as an hour, a day, a month, a year. (Newton's *Scholium,* published in *The Leibnitz-Clarke Correspondence,* 152)

In this passage Newton takes a surprisingly metaphysical turn. Time and space were attributes of a divine being, the ultimate arbiter of the cosmos.

One of the primary objections to Newton's absolute time strikes at the heart of what Newton himself must have grasped as almost divine—that the mathematization of time (and of space) abolishes a past and a future from all calculations, leaving in the wake of this disfranchisement a timeless present.

There are thus two conflicting opinions about time, and they have been around since antiquity. According to Archimedes (and to Parmenides earlier still, for whom ultimate reality is timeless), one must eliminate time, hide it, spirit it away, transform it, reduce it to something else, to geometry, perhaps. Time is an embarrassment. According to Aristotle (and to Heraclitus earlier still, for whom the world is a world of happenings), one must face time squarely, for the world is temporal in its very nature and its comings–into–being are real.

Modern science has largely followed the path of Archimedes rather than that of Aristotle. Time is downplayed, ignored, transformed, eliminated. Cause and effect are replaced by description and relation: do not ask why, but how; the success of the Archimedean program characterizes our scientific dream. (Davis and Hersh 1986, 189–90)

One aspect of the preclusion of time in classical physics has been the tacit assumption of a sort of time symmetry. This symmetry was the product of a mathematical formulation of the past and the future, separated, as they were, into equal portions by an ideal present. In this view the past is something like a future in reverse. Although a sort of time line exists, the Newtonian "observer" was capable of seeing the whole picture: all, in the beauty of geometry and the formalism of mathematics, was given at once. The Newtonian observer had simply to choose which point along his time line—which "present"—was to serve as the ordering focus of his knowledge of the past and future states of his system, that is, the world. Henri Bergson's criticism of this particular vision is trenchant:

And, as physics retained of time only what could as well be spread out all at once in space, the metaphysics that chose the same direction had necessarily to proceed as if time created and annihilated nothing, as if duration had had no efficacy. Bound, like the physics of the moderns and the metaphysics of the ancients, to the cinematographical method, it ended with the conclusion, implicitly admitted at the start and immanent in the method itself: *All is given*. (Bergson 1944, 375)

The analogy to the motion picture is appropriate, though somewhat incomplete, for it is strongly implied in the view of classical physics that the world is just of this order: that we can move back and forth along the time line and stop at any point in order to analyze the state of the world from any given position and deduce the whole from this position.

One of the greatest legacies of Newton (and Galileo) was the ability to count time. As Olivier Costa de Beauregard explains: "before Galileo and Newton, time was not a measurable magnitude. The very possibility of defining time as a measurable magnitude rests on the principle of inertia; that is, on the dynamical relativity principle. No 'scientific revolution' has been greater than this one" (Costa de Beauregard 1987, 23). The nineteenth century was an epoch of movement and of time. The movement was that of birth and generation, not the symmetrical motion of a clocklike universe. At the same time, the century brought forth the greatest flowering of the Newtonian picture. The metaphor is apt, for in this century of unprecedented change Newton's vision—to understand the very mechanism of the cosmos, the one unifying principle with which to determine with absolute certainty our future state—was transposed, by the application of his own principles, into the alien world of the organism, with all the twitches of the living thing. Although the century began in the static, eternal world of the Newtonian mechanism, it was to end in a universe that much more resembled the living form than the clock—a form, moreover, that was moving in one irreversible direction. Time was no longer to be understood as an infinite line intersecting a separate Euclidean space, the mobile T of the physicist moving along it with no predisposition to direction. Time's arrow was shot into the future from an irrevocable past.

New and yet evolving concepts of movement and of time, therefore, were the obvious by-products of this age of direction, as well as the progenitors of its greatest mythology—the idea of progress. This transposition from the Newtonian world was effected by the formulation of two theories and the scientific verification of an old idea. They were: the formulation by Sadi Carnot, Rudolf Clausius, and William Thomson of the so-called second law of thermodynamics; the development of Charles Darwin's theory of evolution; and the verification by James Clerk Maxwell of the constant and finite velocity of light. These singular achievements in our understanding of the nature of the world can well be considered the kingpins in later scientific developments that would greatly alter Newton's premises on a fundamental level. Of significance to the discussion of time in *Camera Lucida* is the fact that these theories are intractably related to an evolving theory of time and its meaning in nature.

Ludwig Boltzmann said of the nineteenth century: "If someone were to ask me what name we should give to this century, I would answer without hesitation that this is the century of Darwin" (quoted in Prigogine and Stengers 1984, 240). Boltzmann's insight seems all the more remarkable in that it comes from a clime so distant from that of biology. One has only to look at Boltzmann's great development of the second law of thermodynamics, however, to grasp his point, for in it there is the beginning of a coalescence between biology and physics so critical to our current understanding of either science as they moved toward a new "symbiosis." But if the nineteenth century is the century of Darwin, then the twentieth century, by a similar extrapolation, is the century of Einstein.

The twentieth century has been a crucible of change. One of the characteristics of this change has been a radical departure from the ways that we have perceived the world. This departure is perhaps best exemplified by prolific developments in the physical sciences. The hegemony of the Newtonian universe was shattered by the work of Einstein, Planck, Heisenberg, Bohr, and others who, led by profound anomalies found within the Newtonian reality, struck out on their own to reshape our perceptions almost at every juncture. Correspondingly, many others from remarkably diverse disciplines seemed to be coming to pointedly similar conclusions about the nature of the world, human existence, and what one might hope to gain of insight from a new vision of the universe and the individual's place in it. And while our view of the world was changing with dizzying and sometimes frightening speed, so was the world itself changing. A few years after the turn of the century the Great War brought to an unalterable end any belief—as mythic as it might have been—in the immutability of the world political order. The great and aged systems of science, philosophy, theology, and government seemed in marked decline and in radical transformation. The years surrounding the turn of the century brought to an end the vestiges of the Enlightenment, and soon this epoch of structured linearity would seem as remote intellectually as did the early Medieval epoch to John Locke and David Hume. The new age, however, was not to be one of expansion but rather one of imposed and perceived limits, which were consistent with our newfound place in the structure of the world.

In a short paper published in 1905 ("Zur Electrodynamik bewegter Kärper" in the *Annalen des Physik,* volume 17, 1905), Einstein proposed his special theory of relativity. With this theory Einstein grasped the significance of the finite velocity of light: that it imposed an absolute limit to our knowledge of the perceptible world. At the same time there was the development by Max Planck of his idea of the discontinuity of matter (quantum theory), which was to alter our vision of the world itself. It can be said with justification that Einstein's theory represents the last step in classical physics, while Planck's work represents the first toward the understanding of a new reality. Although Einstein later repudiated certain of Planck's ideas and attempted, through a "unified field theory," to overcome certain implications of quantum theory (for example, "God does not play dice with the universe," Einstein's oft-quoted renunciation of the stochastical nature of Planck's concept), ironically, he contributed significantly to its development with his own theories on the nature of light.

Hermann Minkowski first proposed the idea of space/time in an address delivered at the 80th Assembly of German Natural Scientists and Physicians in 1908 and was the first to give a geometric expression to Einstein's evolving ideas of time. In his address he states:

> The views of space and time which I wish to lay before you have sprung from the soil of experimental physics, and therein lies their strength. They are radical. Henceforth space by itself, and time itself, are doomed to fade away into mere shadows, and only a kind of union of the two will preserve an independent reality. (Lorentz et al. 1923, 75)

Minkowski's work was to have a profound influence on the further development of the special theory of relativity as it related to time theory. This understanding, although more obvious in relation to so-called cosmological time, applies to any conception of time, regardless of its phenomenology. Knowledge of the world is attained through the signaling of events at the absolute limit of c (the constant and finite velocity of light or electromagnetic force in vacuo); there is always a gap, however small or immeasurable, between the event and our knowledge of it. And even though the knowledge of an event and the event itself can be brought into simultaneity through mathematical deduction (using Einstein's transformation formulas), the natural place of human knowledge of world events is in the past.

With the development of quantum theory, Planck lay the doubt of any possibility of an objective view of reality in the classical sense. Werner Heisenberg moved further in this direction with his principle of indeterminacy, commonly referred to as the "uncertainty principle." With the promulgation of this principle the physicist moved ever farther from the classical physics of Einstein, which seemed to promise, at last, the absolute prediction of the future, into a physics of statistical probabilities—not exactly the prescience that Einstein had in mind.

While the "goal" of the physical sciences has always been predictive in nature (this was, after all, the primary benefit of the Galilean/Newtonian revolution), the goal of Darwinian theory has remained largely retrodictive.

The idea of a randomly evolving system was that which led, in the twentieth century, to a profound understanding of the nature of the world and the importance of time in any intellectual configuration of it. When Hubble first proposed the possibility that the universe was expanding as a whole, the entire nature of physics was transformed, and for the first time it was realized that the universe had a beginning. It was at this point that the second law of thermodynamics took on its present character and when the entropy barrier became its guiding principle. Time was no longer the "embarrassment" of the physicist; full attention was turned to it. Physicist Ilya Prigogine, for example, states in *Order Out of Chaos* that the problem of time has been at the center of his research all his life (Prigogine and Stengers 1984, 10). In Prigogine and Stengers's analysis of the work of Ludwig Boltzmann the notion of time is critical.

> Boltzmann already understood that probability and irreversibility had to be closely related. Only when a system behaves in a sufficiently random way may the difference between past and future, and therefore irreversibility, enter into its description. . . . Indeed, what is the meaning of an arrow of time? The arrow of time is the manifestation of the fact that the future is not given, that, as the poet Paul Valéry emphasized, "time is construction." . . . The recent evolution of physics has emphasized the reality of time. In the process new aspects of time have been uncovered. A preoccupation with time runs all through our century. Think of Einstein, Proust, Freud, Teilhard, Peirce, or Whitehead. (Prigogine and Stengers 1984, 16, 17)

Alfred North Whitehead possessed an acute understanding of the new worldview wrought by the major advances in scientific theory. In his 1929 work, *Process and Reality,* he succinctly states:

> It cannot be too clearly understood that some chief notions of European thought were framed under the influence of a misapprehension, only partially corrected by the scientific progress of the last century. This mistake consists in the confusion of mere potentiality with actuality. Continuity concerns what is potential; whereas actuality is incurably atomic.
> . . . This misapprehension is prompted by the neglect of the principle that, so far as physical relations are concerned, contemporary events happen in *causal* independence of each other. (Whitehead 1930, 95)

In a footnote he elaborates: "This principle lies on the surface of the fundamental Einsteinian formula of the physical continuum" (Whitehead 1930, 95). With the decline of the mechanical view of the world, time has ceased to be the "phantom" of Euclidean space and has taken on the force of the real, the physical entity as it cuts across the "grain of the world," in the words of Eddington.

It is a physical time—exemplified by the work of Einstein, by Planck, and by Clausius—that informs Barthes's vision of the photograph. By extrapolation, it can be argued that the photograph, like light, is a "carnal medium" (which Barthes does contend in *Camera Lucida* [CL 81]). In the photograph the "photographic referent" is linked by the umbilicus of light to the gaze of the observer. It is "the *necessarily* real thing which has been placed before the lens, without which there would be no photograph" (CL 76). Barthes continues:

> Painting can feign reality without having seen it. Discourse combines signs which have referents, of course, but these referents can be and are most often "chimeras." Contrary to these imitations, in Photography I can never deny that *the thing has been there.* There is a superimposition here: of reality and of the past. And since this constraint exists only for Photography, we must consider it, by reduction, as the very essence, the *noeme* of Photography. (CL 76–77)

The indication is evident: this superimposition of reality and of the past produce the causal link, not in a "before" and "after" but given together (as in a double exposure) between referent and image. That the causal link was initiated in a temporal frame (how else does one understand the concept of causation?) but has ceased to reside in such a frame produces an image disorder similar to the one that we *feel* when looking at a double exposure.

If one considers the properties of light as expounded by Einstein, then the photograph—so inextricably connected to light—becomes a sort of signal (again, in the Einsteinian sense). There is a confusion here, and it has always resided in the photograph from its beginning. The confusion is this: in the photograph there is a breaking of the temporal order, a confusion of succession, and this fact is connected with the peculiarities of light and its limiting velocity. In the photograph time is flattened to nothingness, reminiscent of Eddington's famous remark—where the velocity of light is that speed where mass gains infinity; length is shrunk to nothingness; clocks stop as time stands still. Is it part of the uniqueness of the photographic image that it so approximates this condition? Part of the Barthesian quest—his adventure—is in the defining of this approximation. He turns to history:

> The first photographs a man contemplated (Niepce in front of the *dinner table,* for instance) must have seemed to him to resemble exactly certain paintings (still the *camera obscura*); he *knew,* however, that he was nose-to-nose with a mutant . . . ; his consciousness posited the object encountered outside of any analogy, like the ectoplasm of "what-had-been": neither image nor reality, a new being, really: a reality one can no longer touch. (CL 87)

What must it have felt like to have been in the first generation of those who came to know photographs and could remember the time when photographs did not exist? What sort of disorder might this phenomenon have caused in one's perception of reality? The answers to such questions are part of the essence for which Barthes searches.

> Yet I persisted; another, louder voice urged me to dismiss such sociological commentary; looking at certain photographs, I wanted to be a primitive, without culture. So I went on, not daring to reduce the world's countless photographs, any more than to extend several of mine to Photography: in short, I found myself at an impasse and, so to speak, "scientifically" alone and disarmed. (CL 7)

Balzac was such a "primitive." He certainly lived through that period when the photograph, as Barthes asserts, "divides the history of the world" (CL 88). Balzac's observation—the photograph as a type of strange and mysterious emanation—and the fear that possessed him when confronted with the possibility of being "reproduced" were a comment on the new medium of such rarity in his time as to stand apart from the usual arguments as to where photography was to fit in the canon of the arts. Indeed, the precision of which the photograph was capable and the incumbent fidelity of its reproduction of nature were foremost in the minds of most, and this understanding of the new type of image fit comfortably into the general currency of thought throughout most of the nineteenth century. The century was, after all, the first great epoch of precision. Yet it is owing to the precision of the photograph, in part, that there arose a strong argument from those who, like Baudelaire, wanted the photograph to "learn its place"— that of a mechanical contrivance which, however marvelous it might seem, was devoid of the intervening power of the artist's will and intuition and, therefore, had no place in the pantheon of the arts. The debate was launched; Balzac's insight was largely ignored; and what might have been a profound understanding of the significance of the intervention of the photograph in history lay mostly obscured under a patina of arguments as to where this thing, the photograph, was to fit into "the community of images."

Balzac's observation, though outside the pale of debate, was not lost on Baudelaire's "mob." The rapid and burgeoning proliferation of the photograph attests, in part, to a feeling for the new image which must transcend the usual "economic" interpretation of its overwhelming success: that *everyone* could now *afford* to have one's picture made. Witness the thousands of soldiers who flocked to the photographer's studio before they entered battle in the American Civil War. They were not there merely to have their portraits made: there is a palpable reality in these photographs that could never issue from another form of image. We never see paintings or drawings placed on the gravestone when there is a photograph available. The photograph was perceived as a "likeness" in a unique sense, a likeness that partook without mediation of the individual himself. This appears to have been Balzac's insight and his fear, and it is to this insight that Barthes returns in *Camera Lucida.* It is this instinct—felt, intuited, but essentially unarticulated by most of the many thousands who made photography a successful enterprise in its earliest years—that Barthes uses as the binding thread of his book.

Why should, according to Barthes, the advent of photography so decidedly "divide the history of the world"? In confronting this question, one must apprehend the idea of history that possesses Barthes and transforms much of the latter pages of *Camera Lucida:* "Is History," Barthes poses, "not simply that time when we were not born?" (CL 64). As Barthes busies himself with a collection of old family photographs, he ultimately finds one of his mother in which he could read "my nonexistence in the clothes my mother had worn before I can remember her" (CL 64). His ruminations continue:

> Thus the life of someone whose existence has somewhat preceded our own encloses in its particularity the very tension of History, its division. History is hysterical: it is constituted only if we consider it, only if we look at it—and in order to look at it, we must be excluded from it. As a living soul, I am the very contrary of History, I am what belies it, destroys it for the sake of my own history (impossible for me

to believe in "witnesses"; impossible, at least, to be one; Michelet was able to write virtually nothing about his own time). That is what the time when my mother was alive *before me* is—History. . . . No anamnesis could ever make me glimpse this time starting from myself . . . whereas, contemplating a photograph in which she is hugging me, a child, against her, I can waken in myself the rumpled softness of her crêpe de Chine and the perfume of her rice powder. (CL 65)

It is evident here that Barthes possesses a particular and well-defined idea of history. This history is not that of the Greeks or their successors but rather is one born of the Galilean/Newtonian agenda—the exclusion of the observer—and born of the prevailing scientific ideas of the nineteenth century. And if it were to happen that the historian wrote of a time within his own memory, he should nevertheless be compelled to treat this time as though it were of a past beyond his memory—this objectivity is the new standard, the goal. It is this idea of history that Barthes has in mind when he proposes that the nineteenth century gave birth to both history and photography.

It is equally evident that Barthes makes a clear distinction between history and memory. If the past is the undifferentiated texture of all that has been, then the function of history in the past is impositional, impartial; the function of memory is evocational and by its very nature personal. The practice of history developed throughout the nineteenth century—with its mandate toward scientific theory—was perhaps the last attempt to understand the world apart and separate from the newly imposed reality of the photograph. The new history was no longer a simple testament of a time past, a recollection of events, but rather a purposeful attempt to interpret the present by moving retrodictively through the past, imposing upon it an analysis bound to explain the present. Furthermore, it was possessed of a new understanding of time, a real past distinct from the semimythic recollection of unremembered times. History became all-encompassing, reaching well beyond the confines of written testaments. This was the age when the potsherd "spoke" as insistently as the written testament of times long past, and it would eventually show the world the ways to new understandings and the incumbent progress of humanity. History became a social science and played the role of a hard science. Memory was understood to be faulty, but impartial history is certain. Such was the vision of the history developed in the nineteenth century. Little did its progeny suppose that their new science would come to be seen as a different sort of fiction, as laden with mythic creations as any, and as manipulable toward any end in the hands of masters. This has nevertheless been its fate. History, in spite of all its attempts, fails to convince, to affirm a past that cannot be a part of personal memory. Like the painting, it cannot confirm that something has necessarily happened: the event is always optional.

Barthes assumes for the photograph the role of intercession. This intercession cuts across the past at the speed of light and connects it umbilically to our gaze. It is "co-natural" with its referent and, thereby, certifies the reality of the referent. He tells the story of a photograph that he had as a child:

> I remember keeping for a long time a photograph I had cut out of a magazine . . . which showed a slave market: the slavemaster, in a hat, standing; the slaves, in loincloths, sitting. I repeat: a photograph, not a drawing or engraving; for my horror and my fascination as a child came from this: that there was a *certainty* that such a thing had existed: not a question of exactitude, but of reality: the historian was no longer the mediator, slavery was given without mediation, the fact was established *without method*. (CL 80)

Barthes is not asserting that there is no fact verifiable by the "method" of history, only that the photograph is superior as a certificate of the fact. That this is so bears directly upon the unique position held by the photograph in its relation to what we call the past.

There is much confusion about the past. Central to the confusion is the idea of location. Is a thing we have just seen part of the past when we can no longer see it? Most would assume that the existence of the thing is independent of the event of our "seeing" it. This is so because we tend to spatialize knowledge of the present and temporalize knowledge of the past. In other words, we make the assumption *not* that the thing just seen has receded into nonexistence somewhere in the past, but that it or we have changed location. This assumption has the effect of extending the "present" beyond the "event horizon," which is a peculiar way that we have of spatializing time. (It should be added that this time spatialization has no correspondence to Minkowskian space/time.) We think of a thing's having receded into the past as an altogether different event from the thing's change of location and dropping from our sight. After all, we might see the thing again, sometime in the future. But here is implied that the thing *has* receded into the past to return, it is assumed, at some future time. The confusion adheres and is not easily dispelled.

Much of the very nature of the physical sciences has been predictive— this was and remains their primary objective. That this position has been altered somewhat is attributable to the growing importance throughout the nineteenth and twentieth centuries of two retrodictive scientific theories: the second law of thermodynamics and Darwin's theory of evolution. Newtonian (and Einsteinian) dynamics have prepared us psychologically to "look to the future" for any understanding of the world. The "second law" and Darwinism have turned our eyes to the past. The reasons are many but can be summarized as follows: the qualifying fact of the second law of thermodynamics—entropy—has not only given a clearly defined direction to time but has also (with the aid of the development of Boltzmann's theories and quantum mechanics) removed the future from the clearly determinable state represented in classical dynamics to the statistically prob- able state of the increase of entropy. This fact, coupled with the growing interest in "origins," that is, in cosmogony and in evolution, has prepared us to look to the past.

Indeed, our entire perception of the past and its relevance has, since the advent of photography, undergone radical transformation. Yet most of us maintain "ties" to older views in our understanding of the present. Is it our view of the present then, and not of the past, that causes confusion? It was stated earlier that we tend to spatialize the present and to temporalize the past. This penchant might be a natural tendency in our understanding of both. If it is, it is a tendency induced by the psychology of consciousness and not a tendency that can be defended by any extrapolations from the physical reality. Logically, and coincidentally in reality, the present moment (what- ever that may be) and the past are both temporal in their nature. Further- more, the present moment or any "event" therein is physically extentionless. The present of physical reality is the infinitely thin membrane that separates all we know (the past) from that which we portend (the future). There is, in short, a gap between an event and our knowing or observing it. The gap is one of distance and time. It is built into the physiology of our bodies. It is the gap issuing from the finite velocity of light. And it is the *punctum* that pierces through in the photograph and opens a wound.

Although we all "know" what "the present" is (as an expression common to our daily lives), this "knowledge" of the present is bound inextricably to our psychological and physiological makeup and our own innate sense of duration and existence, not from any reasonable understanding of physical reality. This assumption is made on two counts: our biological makeup as living beings and the impossibility of the simultaneity of any event with our knowledge of it. The latter is, as has been noted, a broad implication drawn from the special theory of relativity; the former is perhaps best expressed by Bergson: "Is it not plain that life goes to work here exactly like consciousness, exactly like memory? We trail behind us, unawares, the whole of our past; but our memory pours into the present only the odd recollection or two that in some way complete our present situation" (Bergson 1944, 184). Even earlier in *Creative Evolution* Bergson ties this incursion of the past directly to our sense of duration and its relation to time:

> But as regards the psychical life unfolding beneath the symbols which conceal it, we readily perceive that time is just the stuff it is made of.
>
> There is, moreover, no stuff more resistent nor more substantial. For our duration is not merely one instant replacing another; if it were, there would never be anything but the present—no prolonging of the past into the actual, no evolution, no concrete duration. Duration is the continuous progress of the past which gnaws into the future and which swells as it advances. (Bergson 1944, 6–7)

Bergson represents an interesting chapter in the development of time theory in this century. He carried on a much publicized dispute with Albert Einstein, one that was noted for its virulence. Einstein obviously had Bergson in mind, for example, when he said:

> The only justification for our concepts and system of concepts is that they serve to represent the complex of our experiences; beyond this they have no legitimacy. I am convinced that the philosophers have had a harmful effect upon the progress of scientific thinking in removing certain fundamental concepts from the domain of empiricism, where they are under our control, to the intangible heights of the *a priori*. (Einstein 1956, 2)

Einstein possessed a great dislike for much philosophy of his time. He was not, however, ignorant of its basic arguments and can be considered an admirer of Hume and Berkeley, as well as having taken to heart some of the knottiest complexities to be found in Immanuel Kant—a philosopher with whom he was well acquainted from his youth. Further, it can be argued that certain tenets of quantum theory, particularly Bohr's and Heisenberg's ideas of the observer in science—his or her impact on the physical outcome of any experiment—can be seen as an obscure rapprochement with certain subjectivist philosophies. This point was not missed on Einstein and is, indeed, the source of much of his later arguments against this aspect of quantum theory. Despite Einstein's apparent antipathy, however, Bergson has been somewhat vindicated in the scientific community as the static model of the universe was replaced with the thermodynamic model, a fact which Einstein himself had later to admit. Bergson's ideas on the concreteness of time were groundbreaking and bear directly on the time of human consciousness and its incumbent sense of duration and becoming, so important in the present understanding of the world in the physical sciences.

Thus, for a working definition of *time* as used by Barthes in *Camera Lucida,* it is best compartmentalized (if indeed it can be) into a physical time and a time born of the human consciousness. The idea of a physical time bears directly on all that we know at this point: about the velocity of light and the nature of the limitations that this velocity imposes upon reality and our understanding of it. As noted by Einstein, the very nature of simultaneity (it is assumed here that this concerns *any* expression of simultaneity of observer and the event observed) is that it can only be approximate and that this inexactitude can only be removed by an abstraction (Lorentz et al. 1923, 39). This point is critical to understanding Barthes's explication of the paradox inherent between the photograph and its relationship to time.

In summary, it can be seen that Barthes imposes upon the photograph a unique relation—unique among all classes of images—to a pervasive physical reality. This relation is promulgated upon the inextricable connection of the photograph to the propagation of light and, by extrapolation, a physical time frame as delineated by Einstein in his special theory of relativity, as well as the implications drawn from quantum theory and from the second law of thermodynamics and the irreversible direction of time that it imposes upon the fundamental nature of physical reality.

It can be supposed then that the advent of the photograph, as proposed by Barthes, has changed our understanding of the recent past and has, thereby, introduced a division in history. From the incumbent reordering of our consciousness of the past, the age of the photograph has imparted to history a different and privileged relation to the present. Further, it is assumed here that the conceptual framework of our perception of past, present, future has undergone a radical transformation since the invention of the photograph and its dissemination into our culture, eliciting the "disturbance" to which Barthes alludes.

This disturbance issues from the fact that we who have lived in the time of the photograph live in a privileged position from all those who lived outside this time. This position can be articulated as follows: we can have a *sympathy* for a time outside our memory which was unknown to those who lived before the invention of the photograph. This fact is the defining characteristic of the age of the photograph. "The important thing is that the photograph possesses an evidential force, and that its testimony bears not on the object but on time" (CL 88–89). "The Photograph, for the first time, puts an end to this resistance: henceforth the past is as certain as the present, what we see on paper is as certain as what we touch" (CL 87–88). There is a gap between ourselves and the physical world, and this gap is the effect of the finite velocity of light. Time moves on, and we face the past. This point is the ultimate conclusion of Heisenberg's principle of indeterminacy, which states that we cannot know the position and the velocity of a mass point simultaneously. This "gap" is part of what informs Barthes's sense of the photograph as a wound: the gulf that remains between the photograph's spectrum and its spectator. Yet this gap also asserts the madness that yields "ecstasy."

> Mad or tame? Photography can be one or the other: tame if its realism remains relative, tempered by aesthetic or empirical habits (to leaf through a magazine at the hairdresser's, the dentist's); mad if this realism is absolute and, so to speak, original, obliging the loving and terrified consciousness to return to the very letter of Time: a strictly revulsive movement which reverses the course of the thing, and which I shall call, in conclusion, the photographic *ecstasy*. (CL 119)

The carnality of the photograph is part of its extraordinary power. And this power has indeed transformed our concepts of art and what it means to "do" art. As Benjamin expresses it:

> The nineteenth-century dispute as to the artistic value of painting versus photography today seems devious and confused. This does not diminish its importance, however; if anything, it underlines it. . . .
>   Earlier much futile thought had been devoted to the question of whether photography is an art. The primary question—whether the very invention of photography had not transformed the entire nature of art—was not raised. (Benjamin 1969, 226–27)

Where Barthes might differ markedly from Benjamin is in the latter's concept of the "aura" and an incumbent diminishing—a decay—of the aura through the ubiquity of the photograph. In "A Short History of Photography" Benjamin grants the presence of an aura only to those early portraits that he so obviously admires. It is clear, though, that Benjamin's main concern in "The Work of Art in the Age of Mechanical Reproduction" is in the reproduction of the work of art and not in the photograph itself. In the latter essay he simply maintains that the aura of the original can never be transferred to the photographic image—that this aura is precisely what we lose when we look at a photograph of a painting, for example. Benjamin's aura, however, is one of our perception and feeling for the original work of art; Barthes's "aura" (emanation) is tangible, real, and the photograph, far from "diminishing" it, is the actual proof of it, its ultimate expression. This is so, Barthes maintains, because the photograph *is* a carnal medium, sharing completely with the subject in phenomenal synchrony, a direct relationship to physical reality. The light that emanates from the subject is the same light that creates the latent image on the photographic plate.

If we think of the photograph as somehow analogous to the geometric plotting of phase-space, then the full import of Barthes's assertions is released. Although all photographs represent this analogy, it is more strongly felt in photographs of moving bodies in so-called "time exposures." We are predisposed to regard such images as a distorted reality. In fact, these photographs represent in a graphic way—and drawn from the actual reality that is omnipresent—the precise configuration of a body moving in space-time. This analogy, however, is only partial, for we understand the geometer's plot of phase-space to be a product of logical deduction, which has no direct link to the phenomenal world and is an expression of a mass-point's movement in hypothetical space. Each point along the geometrized trajectory is formulable in terms of "before and after." In a photograph, which is directly connected to the phenomenal world, the direction of this trajectory is wholly obscured. As Barthes puts it: "Time is engorged."

> In the Photograph, Time's immobilization assumes only an excessive, monstrous mode: Time is engorged (whence the relation with the *Tableau Vivant*, whose mythic prototype is the princess falling asleep in *Sleeping Beauty*). That the Photograph is "modern," mingled with our noisiest everyday life, does not keep it from having an enigmatic point of inactuality, a strange stasis, the stasis of an *arrest*. (CL 91)

The important point, however, is that this engorgement of time holds true for all photographic images; it is part of the nature of the photograph.

The engorgement of physical time is the method by which photographs are made. Photographs are pictures of time: they are this before they are anything else. And because this engorgement of time is the necessary condition of each photograph, photographs can be seen as completely atemporal. Any "time" that one ascribes to a photographic image—whether the identification of the period in which the photograph was made or any intuitive feel for the flow and duration of time represented—is time that one puts into the image by way of a secondary interpretation, for the photograph is a picture of the radiant event before the camera and cannot be bound by the usual understanding of time. The photograph is the existential replication by way of infinite repetition of what can have occurred only once.

Barthes's stated quest in *Camera Lucida* is to discover that which sets the photograph apart from all other media. He concludes that it is not his imagination which is stirred by certain photographs but rather it is the physical link through light of the photographed object with himself that confutes his ordered world. In a 1968 essay of the same name Barthes discusses "the reality effect" in literature. In this work he links "objective" physical description (for example, Flaubert's view of Rouen in *Madame Bovary*) with the "concrete detail" and the fragment. Such literary realism resists "meaning"—beyond the mythic confirmation of "what is" (or has been). It is the stuff, Barthes argues, of history, historical discourse. The photograph is again perceived as that which has been developed based on "the incessant need to authenticate the 'real'" (RL 146). The physical trace that the photograph represents to Barthes accords with his concept that "the 'real' is supposed to be self-sufficient, that it is strong enough to belie any notion of 'function,' that its 'speech-act' has no need to be integrated into a structure and that the *having-been-there* of things is a sufficient principle of speech" (RL 147). "Objective" history relies on the reality effect of such techniques (photographs, objects, eyewitnesses, etc.) to compress the figurative distance between signifier and signified, to flatten—so to speak—the package of the sign to a phenomenon resembling a coin whose two sides may show different faces but whose separation is impossible.

Returning in 1972 to the historian Michelet, Barthes comments on Michelet's sense of "event." "The Micheletist fact oscillates between excess of specificity and excess of evanescence; it never has its *exact* dimensions (RL 197). The importance of Michelet's disproportioning of facts lies in its prefiguring of the notion of the detail or the image as that which disrupts the complacency and continuity of classic historicism. For Barthes, Michelet's historical discourse yields pathos and transcends "the mythic opposition between 'subjectivity' and 'objectivity'" (RL 198). As Michelet explains or claims regarding his history of sixteenth-century France: "I believe I have seen this century full in the face, and I have tried to reveal what I have seen. At the least, I have given a true impression of its physiognomy" (MI 101). Michelet also speaks of the value and the uniqueness of the individual and his or her role as guardian of graves.

> Each soul, among vulgar things, possesses certain special individual aspects which do not come down to the same thing, and which must be noted when this soul passes and proceeds into the unknown world.
>
> Suppose we were to constitute a guardian of graves, a kind of tutor and protector of the dead?
>
> I have spoken elsewhere of the duty which concerned Camoëns on the deadly shores of India: *administrator of the property of the deceased.*
>
> Yes, each dead man leaves a small property, his memory, and asks that it be cared for. For the one who has no friends, the magistrate must supply one. For the law, for justice is more reliable than all our forgetful affections, our tears so quickly dried.
>
> This magistracy is History. And the dead are, to speak in the fashion of Roman Law, those *miserabiles personae* with whom the magistrate must be concerned.
>
> Never in my career have I lost sight of that duty of the Historian. I have given many of the too-forgotten dead the assistance which I myself shall require.
>
> I have exhumed them for a second life. . . . Now they live with us, and we feel we are their relatives, their friends. Thus is constituted a family, a city shared by the living and the dead. (MI 101–2)

What may appear to veer toward the sentimental or romantic in Michelet's view of history, nonetheless, serves as foundation for emphasizing the trace of the individual and the agency of the historian in the commingling of the living and the dead. Michelet's as well as Benjamin's discussions of history concern its public face. Barthes's interests in *Camera Lucida* center on its private face. The reality effect can be a tool for manipulation, if that which begins as "exempt of meaning" or as "the real" is caught within a structure or discourse that fails to acknowledge its propagandistic or interpreted "use."

For Barthes photography is not necessarily the rupture that creates history so much as the spatial frame that allows him to enter the coordinates of time. This entering serves not to re-present history—to give it a public face—but to confirm presence—to confirm life as much if not more than to confirm death.

Epilogue: The Photograph and the Postmodern

A paradox: the same century invented History and Photography. But History is a memory fabricated according to positive formulas, a pure intellectual discourse which abolishes mythic Time; and the Photograph is a certain but fugitive testimony; so that everything, today, prepares our race for this impotence: to be no longer able to conceive *duration,* affectively or symbolically: the age of the Photograph is also the age of revolutions, contestations, assassinations, explosions, in short, of impatiences, of every-thing which denies ripening.—And no doubt, the astonishment of "*that-has-been*" will also disappear. It has already disappeared: I am, I don't know why, one of its last witnesses (a witness of the Inactual), and this book is its archaic trace.

Roland Barthes, *Camera Lucida*

The photograph and the postmodern have been linked by many critics and working artists. Photographer Cindy Sherman, for example, offers retakes of certain photographic icons. These retakes not only confute historical time and place but also identity, for she uses herself as model. The sociological rituals that more than a century and a half of photography have engendered become fodder for artist Christian Boltanski. He will appropriate, for example, the images of strangers, whose photographers were usually anony-mous, and re-present a narrative based on his own fancy or ideological interests. The dislocation of these images from their original context into a context of the artist's creation challenges the authenticity of the photograph and its association with truth and the real. The irreversible order in history is disputed at every turn in the photographic works of Sherman and Boltanski: the photograph serves as confuter par excellence because of the common-place belief in the photographic image as record of a specific or concrete time and place.

In his landmark essay "Answering the Question: What is Postmodernism?" Jean-François Lyotard associates the photograph with its ability (along with the cinema) to "accomplish better, faster, and with a circulation a hundred thousand times larger than narrative or pictorial realism, the task that academicism had assigned to realism: to preserve the various consciousnesses from doubt" (Lyotard 1984, 74). The medium of photography serves as a superior tool for those seeking "to stabilize the referent, to arrange it according to a point of view which endows it with a recognizable meaning, to reproduce the syntax and vocabulary which enable the addressee to decipher images and sequences quickly, and so to arrive easily at the consciousness of his own identity as well as the approval which he thereby receives from others" (Lyotard 1984, 74). This view of photography—based as it is on modernity's embrace and exploitation of technology—is precisely what the postmodern artist working with photographs subverts. As Lyotard notes in an article from 1988: "We are no longer at the stage of deploring the 'mechanical reproduction' of works; we know that industry does not mean the end of the arts, but their mutation" (Lyotard 1991, 124).

Postmodern is not a term that entered Barthes's lexicon. American postmodern discourse and its central theoretical influence derive from the Parisian philosophical and intellectual discussions of the last twenty years, but "Foucault rejected the category [of the postmodern]; Guattari despises it; Derrida has no use for it; Lacan and Barthes did not live, and Althusser was in no state to learn about it; and Lyotard found it in America" (Rajchman 1987, 49). Barthes continued, however, to use the term *avant-garde* to express a certain state or quality within the realm of art. In a 1973 essay concerning the painter Réquichot, Barthes reminds us that the avant-garde in art is that which is not classifiable. To name, according to Barthes, is to reassure; the failure to find a name or to classify an object is a laceration.

> From one end of its history to the other, art is merely the varied conflict of image and name: sometimes (at the figurative pole), the exact Name governs and the sign imposes its law upon the signifier; sometimes (at the "abstract" pole—which puts it very badly indeed), the Name escapes, the signifier, continually in explosion, tries to undo the stubborn signified which seeks to return in order to form a sign. (RF 228)

Barthes likens the upsetting of classification to magic: "to aggrandize or simply to change knowledge is to experiment, by certain audacious operations, upon what subverts the classifications we are accustomed to: this is the noble function of magic" (RF 148). And he states that "to be modern is to know *what is no longer possible*" (RF 232).

Barthes's point of view—his emphasis and his selection of words—eludes to one extent or other all categorizations of the postmodern from Lyotard to Jürgen Habermas to Ihab Hassan to Fredric Jameson, and one of the primary reasons for this evasion is Barthes's view of history. Not only does Barthes never name an age that came into being in his own lifetime (he refers to "modern" as an event or cultural turning of the nineteenth century), he admits that "*History* alone institutes the legibility of a writing" (RF 220; emphasis added). Since history, according to Barthes, is that time before he was born, he cannot or chooses not to "read" or "decipher" the contemporary artist's output in terms of a defining schema. In other words, the listing of the schematic differences between modernism and postmodernism, which, for example, Ihab Hassan published in a 1985 article, should strike Barthes not only as meaningless or empty but perhaps even destructive. The words *empty* and/or *destructive* refer not to the consideration of contemporary artists' works but to the closing of their meaning(s)—to the "healing" of the wound(s) they potentially represent.

As one of France's leading cultural commentators throughout most of his adult lifetime, Barthes frequently wrote about contemporary arts and letters. He has long recognized and *named* the existence of the avant-garde. But unlike the terms *modern* and *postmodern,* which have tended to be discussed since the 1980s in formal ways, Barthes simply defines the avant-garde as that which has yet to be recuperated and tamed. So the twentieth century, for example, has been flooded with "avant-garde" art, all of which does not necessarily conform to a broader homogeneity of aesthetic, political, or philosophical concerns.

The term *postmodern* as discussed in the past ten years would probably strike Barthes as "hysterical," just as "History is hysterical: it is constituted only if we consider it, only if we look at it—and in order to look at it, we must be excluded from it" (CL 65). Although Barthes might well agree with Lyotard, who states that photography "stabilizes the referent" in a clearer and faster way than ever before, *Camera Lucida* proffers a reexamination of the medium's unresolved paradox—its lingering laceration. Photography, says Barthes, should not be explored as a question (a theme) but as a wound (CL 21). The wound entails pathos but also desire and ecstasy. While Barthes's distinctions between *the readerly text* and *the writerly text* seem to be analogous to Lyotard's views of the modern versus the postmodern "form," Barthes remains more embroiled than Lyotard in examining the presentation or existence of desire or pathos rather than the medium itself. The photograph, for example, "really transcends itself: is this not," exclaims Barthes, "the sole proof of its art? To annihilate itself as *medium,* to be no longer a sign but the thing itself?" (CL 45). When Barthes speaks of satori or of "an essence (of a wound), what cannot be transformed but only repeated under the instances of insistence (of the insistent gaze)" (CL 49), he emphasizes that which resides in poem, painting, or play that cannot be translated, transformed, or even transliterated.

Barthes argues that first and foremost photography is tied to modernity—not only as an invention, "a clock for seeing"—but also as a new ritual for death.

> for my part I should prefer that instead of constantly relocating the advent of Photography in its social and economic context, we should also inquire as to the anthropological place of Death and of the new image. For Death must be somewhere in a society; if it is no longer (or less intensely) in religion, it must be elsewhere; perhaps in this image which produces Death while trying to preserve life. Contemporary with the withdrawal of rites, Photography may correspond to the intrusion, in our modern society, of an asymbolic Death, outside of religion, outside of ritual, a kind of abrupt dive into literal Death. *Life / Death:* the paradigm is reduced to a simple click, the one separating the initial pose from the final print. (CL 92)

Where one could suggest a modern/postmodern shift in *Camera Lucida* may be in terms of memory versus testimony or reverie versus satori. Barthes, who admires both Michelet and Proust, stresses the points that "History is a memory fabricated according to positive formulas, a pure intellectual discourse which abolishes mythic Time" (CL 93); that "Michelet conceived of History as love's Protest: to perpetuate not only life but also what he called, in his vocabulary so outdated today, the Good, Justice, Unity, etc." (CL 94); that "language is, by nature, fictional" (CL 87), and although photography is "impotent with regard to general ideas (to fiction), its force is nonetheless superior to everything the human mind can or can have conceived to assure us of reality" (CL 87); and that "not only is the Photograph never, in essence, a memory (whose grammatical expression would be the perfect tense, whereas the tense of the Photograph is the aorist), but it actually blocks memory, quickly becomes a counter-memory" (CL 91). According to Barthes time is not recaptured in the photograph; it is *defeated:* "*that* is dead and *that* is going to die" (CL 96). The photograph not only presents an anterior future—"by giving me the absolute past of the pose (aorist), the photograph tells me death in the future" (CL 96)—it does so without mediator: Barthes is the reference of every photograph. Ironically, the certainty of the photograph leaves Barthes feeling increasingly "speechless" about it:

> It is precisely in this *arrest* of interpretation that the Photograph's certainty resides: I exhaust myself realizing that *this-has-been;* for anyone who holds a photograph in his hand, here is a fundamental belief, an "ur-doxa" nothing can undo, unless you prove to me that this image *is not* a photograph. But also, unfortunately, it is in proportion to its certainty that I can say nothing about this photograph. (CL 107)

It perhaps should be argued that modernity has always held the complexities by which some define the postmodern. In terms of photography as a medium, there is no question that Barthes bases his appraisal on that which he believes was always there yet to a large extent remained unarticulated. The photograph is of its time, yet its time did not fully explore the depth of its implications. For Barthes the photograph's madness was ultimately suppressed not only by the arguments as to whether or not photography is an art but also by the analysis characterized by Benjamin that the ubiquity of mechanical reproductions poses questions of authenticity and manipulation. As a living soul, Barthes (so he contends) is the very contrary of history; likewise, the photograph (in its essence) belies or destroys history. Although the evidence of the photograph asserts an important power over history—and Barthes clearly argues this point—he also discerns in certain photographs the "mask vanished," and there remains "a soul, ageless but not timeless" (CL 109). As a form of measurement, time remains in the photograph and connotes the dead; yet paradoxically the very carnality of the photograph betrays a perpetual present that transmits that which is indifferent to the passage of time. As early as 1964, in his essay "Rhetoric of the Image," Barthes notes that with the photograph we have "a new category of space-time: immediately spatial and anteriorly temporal" (RF 33).

Ultimately, Barthes's intellectual interest in the photograph is precisely its modernity. "Film and photography are pure products of the Industrial Revolution. They're not part of a heritage, a tradition" (GV 354). What is "avant-garde" is Barthes's analysis of the medium in *Camera Lucida,* for it displaces the typically "modern" critiques and reinserts the perceptual and, in particular, the temporal hallucination that Barthes avers is either unique to or at least first with the photograph. In the words of William James, Barthes should be considered a "pathfinder":

> What every one can feel, what every one can know in the bone and marrow of him, they [pathfinders, that is, philosophers and poets] sometimes can find words for and express. . . . [Their words and thoughts are] so many spots, or blazes,—blazes made by the axe of the human intellect on the trees of the otherwise trackless forest of human experience. They give you somewhere to go from. (James 1969, 408)

Barthes's own metaphor involves creation and the sowing of seeds:

> Writing is creation, and to that extent it is also a form of procreation. Quite simply, it's a way of struggling, of dominating the feeling of death and complete annihilation. I'm not talking about a belief that as a writer one will be eternal after death, that's not it at all. But, despite everything, when one writes one scatters seeds, one can imagine that one disseminates a kind of seed and that, consequently, one returns to the general circulation of *semences*. (GV 365)

Regardless of the appearance of a search for a system broad enough to analyze all of literature (whether in the form of semiology or linguistics), Barthes must ultimately be seen for the nontotalitarian thinker that he always was. His deemphasis on or turning away from a formal semiology in the 1970s does not vitiate the sincerity or validity of his earlier writings, because Barthes sought to blaze trails not inhabit them, to scatter seeds not tend their growth.

   The seeds of *Camera Lucida* can be discerned, for example, in Marguerite Duras's 1984 novel, *L'Amant* (first published in English in 1985 as *The Lover*). In a work that is haunted by time and its refractions, the photograph provides the kind of imagery and references that Barthes's essay served to evoke. In the novel photographs appear in three forms: the literal ones taken by the narrator's mother or taken by another; the ones that her mother or another failed to take or have taken; and the visual images depicted by the narrator/author that she carries with her in her own mind and memory. Playing off these forms is the tension among the past, present, and future as configured either chronologically, mythically, or creatively. A chronological time line can be traced in the narrative: it embraces the outward life or events of the protagonist from age fifteen and a half to seventeen, from her first meeting with the Chinese lover to their parting. Mythic time, however, pervades the novel as the author (through the persona of the narrator) sets up various organizational or interpretive myths yet never permanently inhabits any one of them. Time as experienced through memory and remembering is creatively integrated with the linear narrative plot—enhancing yet confuting this realistic presentation of event and place. These temporal juxtapositions are intricate and subtle. They suggest the hallucinatory prism that Barthes imparts when simultaneously contemplating the literal death of his mother, his memory of her, and her life before he was born as evidenced by the Winter Garden photograph.

The Lover begins with the evocation of a face. It is the narrator's dual-imaged face; it is the juxtaposition of her face as a young woman versus her face now, which is described as "ravaged." The depiction of her "image" as a young woman is the underlining structural event of the novel. To represent this image is both a literal and figurative enterprise for Duras. Physical appearance through the careful recollection of visual detail constitutes the photograph never taken:

> I think it was during this journey [crossing the river] that the image became detached, removed from all the rest. It might have existed, a photograph might have been taken, just like any other, somewhere else, in other circumstances. But it wasn't. The subject was too slight. Who would have thought of such a thing? The photograph could only have been taken if someone could have known in advance how important it was to be in my life, that event, that crossing of the river. But while it was happening, no one even knew of its existence. Except God. And that's why—it couldn't have been otherwise—the image doesn't exist. It was omitted. Forgotten. It never was detached or removed from all the rest. And it's to this, this failure to have been created, that the image owes its virtue: the virtue of representing, of being the creator of, an absolute. (Duras 1992, 10)

The narrator concomitantly treats this event of crossing a branch of the Mekong as if she were describing a real photographic image and as if she were the creator of the historical image ("This particular day I must be wearing the famous pair of gold lamé high heels. I can't see any others I could have been wearing, so I'm wearing them" [Duras 1992, 11]). She alternates between first-person and third-person reference to herself, the character in the novel. She transplants the photograph never taken with one of her son at age twenty: "His smile strikes me as arrogant, derisive. He's trying to assume the warped image of a young drifter. That's how he likes to see himself, poor, with that poor boy's look, that attitude of someone young and thin. It's this photograph that comes closest to the one never taken of the girl on the ferry" (Duras 1992, 13).

In *The Lover* Duras plays out the Barthesian quandary regarding the portrait-photograph's closed field of forces. "Four image-repertoires intersect here, oppose and distort each other. In front of the lens, I am at the same time: the one I think I am, the one I want others to think I am, the one the photographer thinks I am, and the one he makes use of to exhibit his art. In other words, a strange action: I do not stop imitating myself" (CL 13). The turn of the screw in *The Lover,* however, is that the novelist Duras is both photographer as well as the one being photographed. The interplay of image formation and detachment acts as undercurrent to the waters that shape the narrative. In presenting the experience of reimaging herself at fifteen and a half, the narrator brings forth concrete elements from the past, such as a hat or dress, and in front of the reader constructs not simply a visual image but also an interpreted or mediated portrait that will be reinterpreted several times over in the unfolding of the novel.

> But why was it [the hat] bought? No woman, no girl wore a man's fedora in that colony then. No native woman, either. What must have happened is: I try it on just for fun, look at myself in the shopkeeper's glass, and see that there, beneath the man's hat, the thin awkward shape, the inadequacy of childhood, has turned into something else. Has ceased to be a harsh, inescapable imposition of nature. Has become, on the contrary, a provoking choice of nature, a choice of the mind. Suddenly it's deliberate. Suddenly I see myself as another, as another would be seen, outside myself, available to all, available to all eyes, in circulation for cities, journeys, desire. (Duras 1992, 12–13)

With the intimacy that a first-person narrative evokes, Duras seems never to stop imitating herself: she presents not only the one she thinks she is but also deconstructs the image that she wants others to think she is. At the same time her function as novelist establishes a separation between author and character: Duras, therefore, becomes puppet master to the formation of the narrator's image in service to the author's art.

Similar to Barthes in *Camera Lucida,* the narrator "recognizes" her mother in a certain photograph. Unlike Barthes's Winter Garden photograph, the narrator's photograph contains both her mother and her children, including, of course, the narrator at age four. Unlike Barthes's mother, who did not "suppose" herself in front of the camera, the narrator's mother reveals her discomfort before the lens in "the awkward way she holds herself, the way she doesn't smile, the way she waits for the photo to be over and done with" (Duras 1992, 14). Yet this discomfort is as accurate a representation of the narrator's mother as the sovereign innocence—"the assertion of a gentleness" (CL 69)—that Barthes confronts in his mother's face in the Winter Garden photograph. The essence conveyed of both mothers and the evidence of their presence are equally felt by Barthes and by the narrator in *The Lover.* And as Barthes has already conceded, the photograph does not explain. As Duras's narrator concludes, the just image of her mother is just an image. It cannot explain "what kind of practical consideration made her [mother] leave us like that, every day" (Duras 1992, 14). Was it the recent unnecessary purchase of the house pictured in the photograph? "Or has she just learned she's got the same illness he [her husband] is going to die of? The dates are right" (Duras 1992, 14). Like the photographer of Barthes's Winter Garden portrait, the photographer of "the photo with the despair" (as the narrator describes it) remains unknown. Yet all these points of obscurity and questioning that arise from viewing the print never yield doubt in the narrator's mind as to the reality certified by the photographic image. Duras's own writings, for example, can all too easily distort and misrepresent the events of her life. She indicates this relatively early in *The Lover:* "So you see it wasn't in the bar at Réam, as I wrote, that I met the rich man with the black limousine, it was after we left the land by the dike, two or three years after, on the ferry, the day I'm telling you about, in that light of haze and heat" (Duras 1992, 27). By invoking the realm of photography—of that day being one that should have been photographed—the narrator marks not only the importance of the crossing and subsequent meeting but the extent to which this event is inscribed in her character, in her essence. An image of herself was triggered that day, and its specter has haunted the narrator. The novel seeks not only to capture the specter but to develop it, to begin to comprehend it.

As the novel began, so it concludes—with a return in the last twenty or so pages to the recollection of the narrator's mother and photography. Duras presents a miniature version of part 2 of *Camera Lucida,* in which old family photographs are brought forward and examined. The passage commences by suggesting a sociological interpretation of the ritual of the family photo-graphic portrait. Barthes notes in *Camera Lucida* that this ritual has been analyzed by a team of sociologists as "nothing but the trace of a social protocol of integration, intended to reassert the Family, etc." (CL 7). Duras lingers on this sociology of the family. The narrator notes that the trips to the photographer were an expense, a financial sacrifice, in fact, for her mother. Yet all that this ritual seems to yield are tokens of the family's lack of integration with itself and with society: "We look at them [the family photos], we don't look at each other but we do look at the photographs, each of us separately, without a word of comment, but we look at them, we see ourselves" (Duras 1992, 94). The mother uses the photographs as documents by which to evaluate the health and physical development of her children, but the children never respond to her discussions. The family ritual of having its portrait taken and collectively reviewing the result reveals that "the gulf between us has grown bigger still" (Duras 1992, 94).

In an ironic twist of the innocence and grace that confront and over-whelm Barthes as he views his mother in the Winter Garden photograph, the narrator confronts her own mother's grace and valor in the recollection of her diligence in not only having the family portraits taken but also in carrying them as surrogates for her children to her cousins: "She owes it to herself to do so, so she does, her cousins are all that's left of the family, so she shows them the family photos" (Duras 1992, 96). In this steadfastness—this human, absurd valor—the narrator can see her mother's true grace. In contradistinction, one of the last (if not the last) formal photographic portraits of her mother displays a culturally consistent presentation of the individual and her role in the family. Like the portraits taken of the better-off, elderly natives, her mother's image wears the same expression: "Noble, some would say. Others would call it withdrawn" (Duras 1992, 97). The narrator claims that her mother's expression is the one prepared by profes-sional photographers for all faces in order to confront eternity: "all toned down, all uniformly rejuvenated. . . . This general resemblance, this tact, would characterize the memory of their passage through the family, bear witness at once to the singularity and to the reality of that transit" (Duras 1992, 97). In this context of social uniformity and ritual, a photograph of the narrator crossing the river at fifteen and a half could not be taken. Such an image would have been a record of the narrator's sexual awakening and experimentation with that which is unacceptable in terms of her mother's ideas regarding the family's social class and aspirations. Not only is the picture literally not taken with camera and film, figuratively it has remained undeveloped in the psyche of the narrator until its presentation in this narrative. The novel attests to the narrator's inability to escape the structuring of conventional society. Although the narrator may transgress her mother's and society's norms, her language reveals just how bound to those norms her vision and understanding remain. The photographic journey in this novel, therefore, serves as confirmation that patterns of lineage, class, and gender endure—they are not transcended so much as temporarily eluded.

What unites Barthes and Duras in terms of the photograph is the focus on the medium outside the domain of art. Additionally, it is the portrait that remains central to both texts. The photograph is that literal or even figurative (in the case of the "photograph not taken") entity that grounds the interpretive narrative and links fiction with reality. Duras deliberately seeks a certain tension between what is real and what is fiction in her work *The Lover*, just as Barthes pursues a new form of expression and pathos through "the third form." Although the postmodern artist may perceive photography as a particularly fruitful medium for conveying his or her contemporary sensibility, both Barthes and Duras reserve the photograph as an object, symbol, or metaphor that reflects the modern age of technology and a society that must find a new passage for death. Although the photograph is subject to interpretation and manipulation, its modern power to serve as certifying presence of the past belies the structural and even post-structural fashion to suggest that nothing is real, that everything is constructed. In particular, the private photograph—such as portraits of relatives by obscure photographers—betrays this potential of authentication. For Barthes there is no question that a "just" photograph can serve as proof of his mother's existence. For Duras the certification provided by the photograph appears more complicated. Because the family photographs were performances orchestrated by the narrator's mother to fulfill her perceived familial and class obligations, they immediately testify on two levels: the personal relationship and knowledge between mother and daughter; and the relationship between the individual and her society. Photography offers this potential, but the world of writing—"the elaborations of the text, whether fictional or poetic, . . . is never credible *down to the root*" (CL 97).

In *The Power of Photography* Vicki Goldberg touches upon the future of photography by suggesting that two recent technical developments have effectively sabotaged photography's "truthfulness."

One was the still video camera, which codes images in electronic signals on disks. The photographer can snap a picture, transmit it directly to a computer monitor—perhaps in another city—via telephone line or satellite, then erase the disk, conceivably without ever seeing the picture. Since no record of the photograph exists outside the monitor, whoever controls the computer can theoretically treat the image as a set design and invent a new scenario. (Goldberg 1993, 99)

The second invention is the Scitex machine, a sophisticated computer-imaging system. "Scitex (and Crosfield, and Hell) machines translate any kind of photographic image into electronic signals; from there on, everything can be rearranged at will" (Goldberg 1993, 99). The expanding technology of digital imaging may well obviate the traditional chemistry of photography. Barthes's contention that the astonishment of "that-has-been" will disappear may be more prophetic than he originally intended. In *Camera Lucida* he charges that it has already disappeared, that the book is the archaic trace of the last witness to this astonishment. In fact, the evidentiary power of the traditional photographic processes (both Daguerre's and Talbot's) can be construed as dissipating through the immediate translation of image into electronic signals, whose alteration or manipulation can remain undetectable. With digital imaging the photographic negative will be eliminated, leaving no record by which to analyze such effects as original tonality and to trace such practices as retouching. The photographic madness of which Barthes so piercingly writes in *Camera Lucida* could—with the omnipresence of digital imaging—accede to what the sociologists and semiologists mentioned by Barthes already argue regarding the medium in its traditional form—that there is "no 'reality' . . . nothing but artifice: *Thesis,* not *Physis;* . . . not an *analogon* of the world; what it [the image] represents is fabricated" (CL 88).

Perhaps the contiguity of the publication of *Camera Lucida* with the appearance of new digital technologies has created some of the difficulties of interpretation for the text. Barthes, for example, may appear to mimic Benjamin in the sense of being out of step with one's own time. In "A Short History of Photography" Benjamin clearly prefers the images created during the first twenty years of the medium's public existence as opposed to the photographic work produced through artificial lighting and high-speed film (old versus new technology); Barthes remains focused on the technology of a medium (its chemistry) that is on the brink of extinction as opposed to the image regardless of how it is mechanically "reproduced." In this way Barthes displays a modern not postmodern approach to his topic: his interest and discussion remain grounded in the real and not simply the conceptual. Yet

Barthes's refusal to print the Winter Garden photograph will forever tanta-
lize the reader into speculating that *Camera Lucida* does not derive from the
literal image of his mother and uncle together in the Winter Garden but
from his memory and creativity at play in forging his essay of "the third
form." In a 1994 conference paper entitled "Barthes and the Woman
Without a Shadow," Diana Knight brilliantly and provocatively suggests just
that—that the center of *Camera Lucida* does not, in fact, contain a real
photograph; that the Winter Garden photograph is imaginary. In an age that
hovers over the obsolescence of the imprinting of light on paper or film via
chemical reactions, Barthes's essay can be viewed as the voice of either the
past or the future. Or he may be read with the duality of impulse that has
marked his writings from the beginning.

Bibliography

Andrew, J. Dudley. *The Major Film Theories: An Introduction*. London: Oxford University Press, 1976.

Aristotle. *Metaphysica*. Translated by J. A. Smith and W. D. Ross. Oxford: Clarendon Press, 1908.

―――. *The Physics*. 2 vols. Translated by Philip H. Wicksteed and Francis M. Cornford. London: William Heinemann, 1929.

Arnold, H. J. P. *William Henry Fox Talbot: Pioneer of Photography and Man of Science*. London: Hutchinson Benham, 1977.

The Art of Photography, 1839–1989. New Haven, Conn.: Yale University Press, 1989.

Augustine. *The Confessions of St. Augustine*. Translated by Rex Warner. New York: New American Library, 1963.

Ayer, Alfred J. *The Foundations of Empirical Knowledge*. London: Macmillan, 1959.

―――, ed. *Logical Positivism*. Glencoe, Ill.: Free Press, 1959.

Balzac, Honoré de. *The Works of Honoré de Balzac*. Vol. 11. 1901. Reprint, Freeport, N.Y.: Books for Libraries Press, 1971.

Barrow, Thomas F., Shelley Armitage, and William E. Tydeman, eds. *Reading Into Photography: Selected Essays, 1959–1980*. Albuquerque: University of New Mexico Press, 1982.

Batchen, Geoffrey. "Burning With Desire: The Birth and Death of Photography." *Afterimage* 17, no. 6 (1990): 8–11.

―――. "On Post-Photography." *Afterimage* 20, no. 3 (1992): 17.

Baudelaire, Charles. *Art in Paris, 1845–1862: Salons and Other Exhibitions*. Translated and edited by Jonathan Mayne. Ithaca: Cornell University Press, 1981.

―――. *The Letters of Charles Baudelaire to His Mother, 1833–1866*. Translated by Arthur Symons. New York: Haskell House Publishers, 1971.

―――. *The Painter of Modern Life and Other Essays*. Translated by Jonathan Mayne. [London]: Phaidon, 1964.

Bazin, André. *What is Cinema?* 2 vols. Translated and edited by Hugh Gray. Berkeley: University of California Press, 1967.

Benjamin, Walter. *Illuminations*. Edited by Hannah Arendt. Translated by Harry Zohn. New York: Schocken Books, 1969.

———. "A Short History of Photography." Translated by Phil Patton. *Artforum* 15, no. 6 (1977): 46–51.

Bensmaïa, Réda. *The Barthes Effect: The Essay as Reflective Text.* Translated by Pat Fedkiew. Foreword by Michèle Richman. Minneapolis: University of Minnesota Press, 1987.

Berger, John. *About Looking.* New York: Pantheon Books, 1980.

Bergson, Henri. *Creative Evolution.* Translated by Arthur Mitchell. New York: Modern Library, 1944.

Bernard, Bruce. *Photodiscovery: Masterworks of Photography, 1840–1940.* New York: Abrams, 1980.

Bibliothèque Nationale. *After Daguerre: Masterworks of French Photography (1848–1900).* Translated by Mary S. Eigsti. New York: Metropolitan Museum of Art, 1980.

Blood, Susan. "Baudelaire Against Photography: An Allegory of Old Age." *Modern Language Notes* 101, no. 4 (1986): 817–37.

Bourdieu, Pierre et al. *Photography: A Middle-Brow Art.* Translated by Shaun Whiteside. Stanford, Cal.: Stanford University Press, 1990.

Braive, Michel F. *The Era of the Photograph: A Social History.* Translated by David Britt. London: Thames and Hudson, 1966.

Brentano, Franz. *Philosophical Investigations on Space, Time, and the Continuum.* Translated by Barry Smith. London: Croom Helm, 1988.

Browning, Elizabeth Barrett. *Elizabeth Barrett to Miss Mitford.* Edited by Betty Miller. New Haven, Conn.: Yale University Press, 1954.

Bryson, Norman. *Vision and Painting: The Logic of the Gaze.* London: Macmillan, 1983.

Buckland, Gail. *Fox Talbot and the Invention of Photography.* Boston: Godine, 1980.

Buerger, Janet E. *The Era of the French Calotype.* [Rochester, N.Y.]: International Museum of Photography at George Eastman House, 1982.

Burgin, Victor. *The End of Art Theory: Criticism and Post-modernity.* Atlantic Highlands, N.J.: Humanities Press International, 1986.

———, ed. *Thinking Photography.* London: Macmillan, 1982.

Cadava, Eduardo. "Words of Light: Theses on the Photography of History." *Diacritics* 22, nos. 3–4 (1992): 84–114.

Calvet, Louis-Jean. *Roland Barthes: 1915–1980* (in French). [Paris]: Flammarion, 1990.

Cassirer, Ernst. *Determinism and Indeterminism in Modern Physics: Historical and Systematic Studies of the Problem of Causality.* Translated by O. Theodor Benfey. New Haven, Conn.: Yale University Press, 1956.

———. *The Philosophy of the Enlightenment.* Translated by Fritz C. A. Koelln and James P. Pettegrove. Princeton: Princeton University Press, 1951.

———. *The Problem of Knowledge: Philosophy, Science, and History since Hegel.* Translated by William H. Woglom and Charles W. Hendel. New Haven, Conn.: Yale University Press, 1950.

Champagne, Roland. *Literary History in the Wake of Roland Barthes: Re-defining the Myths of Reading.* Birmingham, Ala.: Summa Publications, 1984.

———. "The Task of Clotho Re-defined: Roland Barthes's Tapestry of Literary History." *L'Esprit Créateur* 22, no. 1 (1982): 35–47.

Coe, Brian. *The Birth of Photography: The Story of the Formative Years, 1800–1900.* New York: Taplinger, 1977.

Comment, Bernard. *Roland Barthes, vers le neutre* (Roland Barthes, towards the neuter). [Paris]: Christian Bourgois, 1991.

Costa de Beauregard, Olivier. *Time, the Physical Magnitude.* Boston: D. Reidel, 1987.

Crawford, William. *The Keepers of Light: A History and Working Guide to Early Photographic Processes.* Dobbs Ferry, N.Y.: Morgan and Morgan, 1979.

Culler, Jonathan. *Barthes.* [London]: Fontana Paperbacks, 1983.

Daval, Jean-Luc. *Photography: History of an Art.* Translated by R. F. M. Dexter. New York: Rizzoli, 1982.

Davis, Philip J., and Reuben Hersh. *Descartes' Dream: The World According to Mathematics.* San Diego: Harcourt Brace Jovanovich, 1986.

Deleuze, Gilles. *Cinema 2: The Time-Image.* Translated by Hugh Tomlinson and Robert Galetta. Minneapolis: University of Minnesota Press, 1989.

Delord, Jean. *Roland Barthes et la photographie* (Roland Barthes and the photograph). Paris: Créatis, 1981.

Derrida, Jacques. "Les morts de Roland Barthes" (The deaths of Roland Barthes). *Poétique* 47 (1981): [269]–92.

Descartes, René. *The Philosophical Works of Descartes.* Vol. 1. Translated by Elizabeth S. Haldane. Cambridge: Cambridge University Press, 1973.

Diamond, Josephine. "Baudelaire's Exposure to the Photographic Image." *Art Criticism* 2, no. 2 (1986): 1–10.

Duras, Marguerite. *The Lover.* Translated by Barbara Bray. New York: HarperCollins, 1992.

Ebersole, Frank B. *Things We Know: Fourteen Essays on Knowledge.* Eugene: University of Oregon Books, 1967.

Eddingon, A. S. *The Nature of the Physical World.* New York: Macmillan, 1929.

Edelman, Gerald M. *Bright Air, Brilliant Fire: On the Matter of Mind.* New York: Basic Books, 1992.

————. *The Remembered Present: A Biological Theory of Consciousness.* New York: Basic Books, 1989.

Eder, Joseph Maria. *History of Photography.* Translated by Edward Epstean. New York: Columbia University Press, 1945.

Einstein, Albert. *Essays in Science.* Translated by Alan Harris. New York: Philosophical Library, [1955?] circa 1934.

————. *The Meaning of Relativity.* Princeton: Princeton University Press, 1956.

Einstein, and Leopold Infeld. *The Evolution of Physics.* New York: Simon and Schuster, 1938.

Fouque, Victor. *The Truth Concerning the Invention of Photography: Nicéphore Niépce, His Life, Letters and Works.* Translated by Edward Epstean. 1935. Reprint, New York: Arno Press, 1973.

Freund, Gisèle. *Photography and Society.* Boston: Godine, 1982.

Gernsheim, Helmut. *The Origins of Photography.* New York: Thames and Hudson, 1982.

Gernsheim, and Alison Gernsheim. *The History of Photography: From the Camera Obscura to the Beginning of the Modern Era.* New York: McGraw-Hill, 1969.

————. *L. J. M. Daguerre: The History of the Diorama and the Daguerreotype.* London: Secker and Warburg, 1956.

Gilman, Margaret. *Baudelaire the Critic.* New York: Columbia University Press, 1943.

Goldberg, Vicki, ed. *Photography in Print: Writings from 1816 to the Present.* New York: Simon and Schuster, 1981.

————, ed. *The Power of Photography: How Photographs Changed Our Lives.* New York: Abbeville Publishing Group, 1993.

Gosling, Nigel. *Nadar.* New York: Knopf, 1976.

Greaves, Roger. *Nadar ou le paradoxe vital* (Nadar or the vital paradox). Paris: Flammarion, 1980.

Habermas, Jürgen. *The Philosophical Discourse of Modernity: Twelve Lectures.* Translated by Frederick Lawrence. Cambridge, Mass.: MIT Press, 1987.

Hammond, John H., and Jill Austin. *The Camera Lucida in Art and Science.* Bristol, U.K.: Adam Hilger, 1987.

Hammond, Mary Sayer. "The Camera Obscura: A Chapter in the Pre-history of Photography." Ph.D. diss., Ohio State University, 1986. Ann Arbor, Mich.: University Microfilms International, 1988.

Harvey, David. *The Condition of Postmodernity: An Enquiry into the Origins of Cultural Change.* Oxford: Basil Blackwell, 1989.

Hawking, Stephen W. *A Brief History of Time: From the Big Bang to Black Holes.* New York: Bantam Books, 1988.

Haworth-Booth, Mark. *The Golden Age of British Photography, 1839–1900.* Philadelphia: Aperture, 1984.

Heidegger, Martin. *History of the Concept of Time.* Translated by Theodore Kisiel. Bloomington: Indiana University Press, 1985.

Heisenberg, Werner. *Physics and Beyond: Encounters and Conversations.* Translated by Arnold J. Pomerans. New York: Harper Torchbooks, 1972.

———. *Physics and Philosophy: The Revolution in Modern Science.* New York: Harper and Brothers, 1958.

Hickman, Larry. "Experiencing Photographs: Sontag, Barthes, and Beyond." *Journal of American Culture* 7, no. 4 (1984): 69–72.

Hiley, B. J., and F. David Peat, eds. *Quantum Implications: Essays in Honor of David Bohm.* London: Routledge, 1991.

Husserl, Edmund. *The Phenomenology of Internal Time-Consciousness.* Edited by Martin Heidegger. Translated by James S. Churchill. Bloomington: Indiana University Press, 1964.

Hutcheon, Linda. *The Politics of Postmodernism.* London and New York: Routledge, 1989.

James, William. *Collected Essays and Reviews.* New York: Russell and Russell, 1969.

Jammes, André, and Eugenia Parry Janis. *The Art of French Calotype.* Princeton: Princeton University Press, 1983.

Jussim, Estelle. *The Eternal Moment: Essays on the Photographic Image.* New York: Aperture, 1989.

Kant, Immanuel. *Prolegomena.* Translated by Paul Carus. La Salle, Ill.: Open Court Publishing, 1990.

Kelly, Jill Beverly. "The Relationship of Photography to the French Literary Realism of the Nineteenth Century: The Novelist as a Tourist of Reality." Ph.D. diss., University of Oregon, 1982. Ann Arbor, Mich.: University Microfilms International, 1984.

Ken, Alexandre. *Dissertations historiques, artistiques et scientifiques sur la photographie* (Historical, artistic, and scientific writings on the photograph). 1864. Reprint, New York: Arno Press, 1979.

Kozloff, Max. *The Privileged Eye: Essays on Photography.* Albuquerque: University of New Mexico Press, 1987.

Krauss, Rosalind E. *The Originality of the Avant-Garde and Other Modernist Myths.* Cambridge, Mass.: MIT Press, 1985.

————. "Tracing Nadar." In *Reading Into Photography: Selected Essays, 1959–1980,* edited by Thomas F. Barrow, Shelley Armitage, and William E. Tydeman, 117–34. Albuquerque: University of New Mexico Press, 1982.

Kurzweil, Edith. *The Age of Structuralism: Lévi-Strauss to Foucault.* New York: Columbia University Press, 1980.

la Croix, Arnaud de. *Barthes: pour une éthique des signes* (Barthes: for an ethic of signs). Bruxelles: De Boeck-Wesmael s.a., 1987.

Lacan, Jacques. *Écrits: A Selection.* Translated by Alan Sheridan. New York: Norton, 1977.

Lavers, Annette. *Roland Barthes: Structuralism and After.* Cambridge, Mass.: Harvard University Press, 1982.

Leibniz, Gottfried Wilhelm. *The Leibniz-Clarke Correspondence.* Edited by H. G. Alexander. Manchester, U.K.: Manchester University Press, 1956.

Lombardo, Patrizia. *The Three Paradoxes of Roland Barthes.* Athens: University of Georgia Press, 1989.

Lorentz, H. A. *Collected Papers.* Vol. 4. The Hague: Martinus Nijhoff, 1937.

Lorentz, H. A., A. Einstein, H. Minkowski, and H. Weyl. *The Principle of Relativity.* Translated by W. Perrett and G. B. Jeffery. New York: Dodd, Mead, 1923.

Lyotard, Jean-François. *The Inhuman: Reflections on Time.* Translated by Geoffrey Bennington and Rachel Bowlby. Stanford, Cal.: Stanford University Press, 1991.

————. *The Postmodern Condition: A Report on Knowledge.* Translated by Geoff Bennington and Brian Massumi. Minneapolis: University of Minnesota Press, 1984.

Maxwell, J. Clerk. *Matter and Motion.* New York: Dover Publications, [1951].

Melkonian, Martin. *Le corps couché de Roland Barthes* (The sleeping body of Roland Barthes). Paris: Librarie Séguier, 1989.

Metz, Christian. *Film Language: A Semiotics of the Cinema.* Translated by Michael Taylor. New York: Oxford University Press, 1974.

Miller, D. A. *Bringing Out Roland Barthes.* Berkeley: University of California Press, 1992.

Moriarty, Michael. *Roland Barthes.* Stanford, Cal.: Stanford University Press, 1991.

Morris, Wright. *Time Pieces: Photographs, Writing, and Memory.* New York: Aperture, 1989.

Nadar. *Quand j'étais photographe* (When I was a photographer). Paris: Flammarion, [1899?].

Nadar; Les années créatrices: 1854–1860 (Nadar; the creative years: 1854–1860). Paris: Editions de la Réunion des musées nationaux, 1994.

Newhall, Beaumont. *The History of Photography: From 1839 to the Present Day.* New York: Museum of Modern Art, 1964.

Pagels, Heinz R. *Perfect Symmetry: The Search for the Beginning of Time.* New York: Simon and Schuster, 1985.

Le Paris souterrain de Félix Nadar: 1861 (The underground Paris of Félix Nadar: 1861). Paris: Caisse Nationale des Monuments Historiques et des Sites, 1982.

Pichois, Claude, and Jean-Paul Avice. *Baudelaire: Paris* (in French). [Paris]: Editions Paris-Musées/Quai Voltaire, 1993.

Planck, Max. *The New Science.* Translated by James Murphy and W. H. Johnston. [New York]: Meridian Books, [1959].

————. *A Survey of Physics: A Collection of Lectures and Essays.* Translated by R. Jones and D. H. Williams. New York: E. P. Dutton, [1925].

Potonniée, Georges. *The History of the Discovery of Photography.* Translated by Edward Epstean. 1936. Reprint. New York: Arno Press, 1973.

Prigogine, Ilya, and Isabelle Stengers. *Order Out of Chaos: Man's New Dialogue with Nature*. New York: Bantam Books, 1984.

Quine, W.V. *Ontological Relativity and Other Essays*. New York: Columbia University Press, 1969.

————. *Theories and Things*. Cambridge, Mass.: Belknap Press, 1981.

Rabaté, Jean-Michel. *La Beauté amère: fragments d'esthetiques* (The bitter beauty: fragments of aesthetics). Seyssel, France: Champ Vallon, 1986.

Rajchman, John. "Postmodernism in a Nominalist Frame: The Emergence and Diffusion of a Cultural Category." *FlashArt* no. 137 (1987): 49–51.

Raser, Timothy. *A Poetics of Art Criticism: The Case of Baudelaire*. Chapel Hill: University of North Carolina Press, 1989.

Reichenbach, Hans. *The Direction of Time*. Edited by Maria Reichenbach. Berkeley: University of California Press, 1956.

Rice, Donald, and Peter Schofer. "S/Z: Rhetoric and Open Reading." *L'Esprit Créateur* 22, no. 1 (1982): 20–34.

Rice, Shelley. "Souvenirs." *Art in America* 76, no. 9 (1988): 156–71.

Richard, Jean-Pierre. "Nappe, charnière, interstice, point" (in French). *Poétique* 47 (1981): [293]–302.

Robinson, John Mansley. *An Introduction to Early Greek Philosophy*. Boston: Houghton Mifflin, 1968.

Roger, Philippe. *Roland Barthes, roman* (Roland Barthes, novel). [Paris]: Editions Grasset & Fasquelle, 1986.

Roland Barthes et la photo: le pire des signes (Roland Barthes and the photo: the worst of signs). [Paris]: Contrejour, 1990.

Rudisill, Richard. *Mirror Image: The Influence of the Daguerreotype on American Society*. Albuquerque: University of New Mexico Press, 1971.

Ryle, Gilbert. *The Concept of Mind*. New York: Barnes & Noble, 1949.

Sarkonak, Ralph. "Roland Barthes and the Spectre of Photography." *L'Esprit Créateur* 22, no. 1 (1982): 48–68.

Sartre, Jean-Paul. *The Psychology of the Imagination*. Secaucus, N.J.: Citadel Press, [1961, circa 1948].

Scharf, Aaron. *Art and Photography*. London: Penguin Press, 1968.

Schilpp, Paul Arthur, ed. *Albert Einstein: Philosopher-Scientist*. Vol. 1. New York: Harper Torchbooks, 1951.

Schrödinger, Erwin. *Mind and Matter*. Cambridge, U.K.: University Press, 1959.

Schwarz, Heinrich. *Art and Photography: Forerunners and Influences*. Rochester, N.Y.: Visual Studies Workshop Press, 1985.

Sobieszek, Robert, ed. *The Prehistory of Photography: Five Texts*. New York: Arno Press, 1979.

Sontag, Susan. *On Photography*. New York: Farrar, Straus & Giroux, 1977.

Starkie, Enid. *Baudelaire*. London: Faber and Faber, [1957].

Stenger, Erich. *The History of Photography: Its Relation to Civilization and Practice*. Translated by Edward Epstean. 1939. Reprint. New York: Arno Press, 1979.

The Stoic and Epicurean Philosophers: The Complete Extant Writings of Epicurus, Epictetus, Lucretius, and Marcus Aurelius. New York: Modern Library, 1940.

Talbot, William Henry Fox. *The Pencil of Nature.* 1844, 1846. Facsimile. New York: Da Capo Press, 1969.

Thomas, David Bowen. *'From today painting is dead': The Beginnings of Photography.* [London]: Arts Council of Great Britain, [1972].

Todorov, Tzvetan. "The Last Barthes." Translated by Richard Howard. *Critical Inquiry* 7, no. 3 (1981): 449–54.

Trachtenberg, Alan, ed. *Classic Essays on Photography.* New Haven, Conn.: Leete's Island Books, 1980.

Ungar, Steven. *Roland Barthes: The Professor of Desire.* Lincoln: University of Nebraska Press, 1983.

Ungar, and Betty R. McGraw, eds. *Signs in Culture: Roland Barthes Today.* Iowa City: University of Iowa Press, 1989.

Weaver, Mike, ed. *The Art of Photography: 1839–1989.* New Haven, Conn.: Yale University Press, 1989.

Wexler, Laura Jane. "The Puritan in the Photograph." Ph.D. diss., Columbia University, 1986. Ann Arbor, Mich.: University Microfilms International, 1986.

Whitehead, Alfred North. *Process and Reality: An Essay in Cosmology.* Cambridge, U.K.: University Press, 1930.

———. *Science and the Modern World: Lowell Lectures, 1925.* New York: Macmillan, 1947.

Wiseman, Mary Bittner. *The Ecstasies of Roland Barthes.* New York: Routledge, 1989.

Wittgenstein, Ludwig. *Philosophical Investigations.* Translated by G. E. M. Anscombe. New York: Macmillan, 1953.

———. *Tractatus Logico-Philosophicus.* Translated by C. K. Ogden. London: Routledge, 1990.

Wood, John, ed. *The Daguerreotype: A Sesquicentennial Celebration.* Iowa City: University of Iowa Press, 1989.

Index